U.S. Department of Justice
Office of the Inspector General
Evaluation and Inspections Division

Enhanced Screening of
BOP Correctional Officer Candidates
Could Reduce Likelihood of Misconduct

September 2011

I-2011-002

EXECUTIVE DIGEST

INTRODUCTION

The Office of the Inspector General (OIG) conducted this review to examine whether the Federal Bureau of Prisons' (BOP) hiring process could more effectively identify potentially unsuitable applicants for Correctional Officer positions. As part of our review, we evaluated whether the BOP could use selected background characteristics as indicators of future Correctional Officer conduct when assessing applicants' suitability.

While most of the BOP's 16,000 Correctional Officers never engage in misconduct or commit crimes, those who do jeopardize the safety and security of other staff and inmates and undermine public confidence in the BOP. From fiscal year (FY) 2001 through FY 2009, an average of 113 officers per year committed misconduct resulting in at least a 1-day suspension. Further, for each Correctional Officer terminated due to arrest or misconduct, or who resigns under inquiry, the BOP bears the cost of hiring and training a new Correctional Officer – approximately $66,650 for the first year.

The BOP's hiring process seeks to identify qualified and suitable Correctional Officer applicants who possess qualities that are difficult to measure, such as integrity, decision-making ability, and judgment. Correctional Officers must also be capable of employing appropriate levels of force and persuasion to control inmates, and recognize and resist inmate attempts at manipulation. Before making a conditional offer of employment, the BOP assesses applicants' suitability through a series of steps that include a pre-employment interview, a panel interview, and credit and criminal records checks. Information provided by applicants is compared against 30 measurable thresholds in the BOP's Guidelines of Acceptability. If an applicant exceeds any one Guideline threshold, the applicant is considered unsuitable and can only be hired if the BOP grants a waiver.

A successful applicant who accepts a conditional offer of employment begins work in a BOP prison for a 12-month probationary period. As soon as the conditional offer of employment is made, the BOP requests that the Office of Personnel Management (OPM) conduct a background investigation on the new employee. The BOP attempts to adjudicate the results of that background investigation before the Correctional Officer completes the 12-month probationary period and becomes a permanent employee. If the results of the background investigation are negative or the BOP discovers a Correctional Officer has been dishonest in the information he or she provided to the BOP prior to being hired, the BOP can terminate the officer. Terminating a probationary employee is easier than terminating a permanent employee.[1]

The OIG's review employed a multi-disciplined approach that included evaluating hiring policies, interviews, site visits, and statistical procedures, including classification tree and logistic regression analyses, which find relationships among variables and provide more accurate predictions. We focused on Correctional Officers' conduct in their first 2 years of service with the BOP, but we analyzed misconduct and arrest data for FY 2001 through FY 2010 to identify trends involving newly hired Correctional Officers. We analyzed background information for approximately 12 percent of the 3,731 Correctional Officers hired by the BOP during FY 2007 and FY 2008 to identify any characteristics that correlated to future conduct.

RESULTS OF THE REVIEW

Misconduct allegations and arrests of BOP Correctional Officers have increased in the last decade.

The number of misconduct investigations of BOP Correctional Officers doubled from FY 2001 to FY 2010, rising from 2,299 to 4,603. Correctional Officers were investigated disproportionately to their representation in the BOP workforce throughout the decade, in that while they accounted for approximately 40 percent of BOP staff, they were the subject of 53 percent of the misconduct allegations in FY 2001 and 63 percent of the allegations in FY 2010. Of the 32,455 misconduct allegations made against Correctional Officers between FY 2001 and FY 2009 for which there were final resolutions, 16,717 (52 percent) were substantiated.

---

[1] Probationary employees terminated for pre-employment reasons receive 10 days' advance written notice and an opportunity to refute the reasons for termination. Probationary employees also receive limited appeal rights to the Merit Systems Protection Board (MSPB). In contrast, permanent employees terminated for pre-employment reasons receive 30 days' advance written notice with an opportunity to refute the reasons for termination. Permanent employees also receive full, union-negotiated appeal rights to the MSPB or the option of filing a formal complaint with the Equal Employment Opportunity Commission.

Arrests of Correctional Officers as a result of substantiated allegations of criminal conduct have also increased. From FY 2001 through FY 2010, a total of 272 Correctional Officers were arrested, rising 89 percent from 18 in FY 2001 to 34 in FY 2010. Correctional Officer staffing levels at the BOP during the same time period rose only 24 percent.

Misconduct allegations and arrests are most common in Correctional Officers' early years.

Over half (58 percent) of the Correctional Officers who had substantiated allegations of misconduct, and who received discipline of at least a 1-day suspension between FY 2001 and FY 2009, were disciplined for conduct that occurred within their first 2 years of service with the BOP. We identified 1,020 Correctional Officers hired during that time period who had had substantiated misconduct allegations, such as physical abuse of an inmate or misuse of government computers, resulting in at least a 1-day suspension. Of those 1,020 Correctional Officers, 587 were disciplined for behavior that occurred within 2 years of their start dates.

When we analyzed arrest data for FY 2001 through FY 2010, we found that of the 272 Correctional Officers arrested, over one-quarter (27 percent) were arrested for behavior that took place during their first 2 years of service. Types of behavior for which arrests were made included introduction of an illegal substance into a prison and having a sexual relationship with an inmate.

Classification tree, conditional inference tree, and logistic regression analyses show combinations of applicants' background characteristics are predictive of bad behavior, but the BOP's hiring process does not have a systematic method of evaluating combinations.

Extensive classification tree, conditional inference tree, and logistic regression analyses the OIG conducted found that combinations of certain applicant characteristics have strong relationships with an increased likelihood of substantiated misconduct resulting in at least a 1-day suspension during the first 2 years after a Correctional Officer begins work.[2] Of the 175 Correctional Officer characteristics we analyzed, 2 predicted a greater likelihood of good behavior and did so

---

[2] See Appendix III for a detailed discussion of our methodology and analysis.

independently of other characteristics: educational level and duration of the longest civilian job previously held. While we are not making any recommendations related to education requirements, we believe the BOP should consider the predictive relationship established by our analysis between good conduct and officers with at least some college-level education when determining goals for the desired makeup of the BOP's Correctional Officer workforce.

Seven other characteristics predicted a higher likelihood that Correctional Officers would commit substantiated misconduct resulting in at least a 1-day suspension within the first 2 years of being hired if the characteristics appeared in particular combinations. In the body and appendices of this report, we discuss the combinations uncovered by our tree analysis and logistic regression analysis. It is important to note that the specific characteristics that make up the combinations matter less than the fact that our analyses established that combinations matter. Indeed, any combinations the BOP adopts would likely not be identical to ours. Instead, if the BOP assesses the value of using combinations in its screening practices and decides to implement a composite scoring system, the system would include the BOP's own analysis and judgment and would be used in conjunction with or incorporated into the Guidelines of Acceptability.

The BOP's current system does not include a mechanism for systematically considering combinations of characteristics and assigning weights to derive a risk factor when deciding whether to hire or make a Correctional Officer a permanent member of the BOP's staff. If the BOP were to systematically evaluate individuals based on combinations of factors in addition to the single thresholds it now relies on, it could add a useful tool to its screening practices.

Potential Benefits of Composite Scoring

To provide a tangible estimate of the benefits of a composite scoring mechanism, we performed an additional analysis to find how many of the Correctional Officers in our sample would have been identified by the three predictive combinations that surfaced in our analyses. This was an analysis based on the findings of the classification tree, conditional inference tree, and logistic regression analyses, but performed separately. We found that, based on our sample, the tangible benefits of the BOP using composite scoring to assess Correctional Officer applicants could be substantial. Specifically, the 3 predictive combinations would have identified 67 out of 171 Correctional Officers in our sample who committed substantiated misconduct resulting in at least a 1-day suspension. In contrast, the 3 predictive combinations would have identified only 32 out of 287 Correctional Officers who did not commit misconduct.[3] Thus, the combinations would have been a useful tool in assessing Correctional Officer applicants in our sample and, consequently, enhancing the safety and security of the prisons in which the 67 identified Correctional Officers were hired.[4]

Our additional analysis also found that the BOP could realize cost savings by using composite scoring to identify Correctional Officers who are more likely than others to commit misconduct. Correctional Officers that are terminated due to misconduct or resign during misconduct inquiries force the BOP to expend resources hiring and training replacement officers. Taken together, the 3 combinations detailed above would have identified 41 Correctional Officers in our sample who were terminated due to misconduct or resigned during misconduct inquiries. Had the BOP not hired those officers, it would have represented a cost savings to the BOP for items such as training, overtime paid to staff covering shifts of the departed Correctional Officers, additional hours of administrative work by BOP support staff, OPM background investigations, equipment and uniforms, and drug screening.

The BOP reduced the possibility of permanently hiring unsuitable Correctional Officers by shortening the amount of time taken to adjudicate background investigations.

Ensuring the timely adjudication of background investigations is essential because if derogatory information is uncovered during the employees' probationary period, it is easier for the BOP to terminate them. Once employees complete their probationary periods, they have the full bargaining unit appeal rights of permanent employees. We found the percentage of Correctional Officer background investigations completed after the 12-month probationary year ended decreased from 43 percent and 44 percent in FY 2007 and FY 2008, respectively, to 14 percent in FY 2009 and 6 percent in FY 2010.

---

[3] Any screening factors, including those currently found in the BOP's Guidelines of Acceptability, eliminate some applicants who will never commit misconduct along with applicants who will.

[4] Because the population of Correctional Officers we drew our sample from did not include the applicants who had already been screened out by the BOP's Guidelines of Acceptability, it was not possible to estimate the additional number of applicants from that population who would have met the criteria of one or more of the combinations.

The BOP official in charge of background investigation adjudication attributed the decrease to three primary reasons. First, OPM decreased the amount of time it took to conduct investigations. Second, the BOP added 6 positions to the unit responsible for adjudications, bringing the total number of employees to 32. Third, that unit assigns a specially designated team to the adjudications of employees who have completed 10 months of their 12-month probationary periods in an effort to finalize the adjudications before the probationary periods end.

CONCLUSION AND RECOMMENDATION

The BOP's improvement in the timely adjudication of background investigations has put it in a stronger position to remove unsuitable Correctional Officers before they become permanent employees. To further reduce the likelihood of Correctional Officer misconduct and arrests, particularly within the first 2 years of being hired, the BOP could consider additional ways of assessing applicants. Currently, the BOP's system does not include a mechanism for assigning weights and systematically considering combinations of characteristics to derive a risk factor when deciding whether to make a newly hired Correctional Officer a permanent member of the staff. The proof of concept demonstrated by our statistical procedures and logistic regression analysis found that combinations of applicants' characteristics are predictive of future conduct. We believe the BOP should assess the value of establishing a composite scoring system for evaluating Correctional Officer applicant suitability.

We recommend that the BOP:

1. Consider developing a composite scoring mechanism for assessing the suitability of Correctional Officer applicants.

TABLE OF CONTENTS

BACKGROUND 1

SCOPE AND METHODOLOGY OF THE OIG REVIEW 9

RESULTS OF THE REVIEW 11

Misconduct allegations and arrests of BOP Correctional Officers
have increased in the last decade. 11

Misconduct allegations and arrests are most common in
Correctional Officers' early years. 15

Classification tree and logistic regression analyses show
combinations of applicants' background characteristics are
predictive of bad behavior, but the BOP's hiring process does not
have a systematic method of evaluating combinations. 18

The BOP reduced the possibility of permanently hiring unsuitable
Correctional Officers by shortening the amount of time taken to
adjudicate background investigations. 26

CONCLUSIONS AND RECOMMENDATION 28

APPENDIX I: OIG METHODOLOGY FOR THIS REVIEW 30

APPENDIX II: VARIABLES COLLECTED DURING FILE REVIEW 36

APPENDIX III: REGRESSION ANALYSIS METHODOLOGY 43

APPENDIX IV: THE BOP'S HIRING AND SELECTION PROCESS 59

**APPENDIX V: STATE DEPARTMENT OF CORRECTIONS
QUESTIONNAIRE** 65

APPENDIX VI: THE BOP's RESPONSE TO DRAFT REPORT 68

APPENDIX VII: OIG ANALYSIS OF THE BOP's RESPONSE 70

BACKGROUND

The Office of the Inspector General (OIG) conducted this review to examine whether the Federal Bureau of Prisons' (BOP) hiring process can be made more effective in identifying potentially unsuitable applicants for Correctional Officer positions. We also evaluated whether the BOP could use selected background characteristics of BOP Correctional Officers as indicators of future conduct when assessing applicants' suitability. Correctional Officers represent the largest category of BOP employees nationwide. These officers help provide custody and control over a federal inmate population that numbered more than 216,000 as of July 2011 and is growing each year. At the end of fiscal year (FY) 2010, the 16,009 Correctional Officers made up 42 percent of the 38,039 full-time employees.

During FY 2010, the BOP received 30,052 applications for the Correctional Officer position and hired 1,939. The BOP's hiring process seeks to identify qualified and suitable Correctional Officer applicants who possess qualities that are difficult to measure, such as integrity, decision-making ability, and judgment. Correctional Officers must also be capable of employing appropriate levels of force and persuasion to control inmates, and recognize and resist inmate attempts at manipulation.

While most BOP Correctional Officers never engage in misconduct or commit crimes, those who do jeopardize the safety and security of other staff and inmates, and undermine public confidence in the BOP. From FY 2001 through FY 2009, an average of 113 officers per year committed misconduct resulting in at least a 1-day suspension. Further, for each Correctional Officer terminated due to arrest or misconduct, or who resigns under inquiry, the BOP bears the cost of hiring and training a new Correctional Officer – approximately $66,650 for the first year.

Misconduct and Crimes

The BOP defines the on-duty and off-duty conduct for which employees can be disciplined, ranging from severe behavior, such as a life-threatening physical assault on an inmate, to minor behavior, such as using profanity while on duty. If an employee is suspected of violating these standards of conduct or federal or state law, a complaint of employee misconduct is filed with the BOP's Office of Internal Affairs or

U.S. Department of Justice   1
Office of the Inspector General
Evaluation and Inspections Division

the OIG.[5] All allegations of misconduct within the BOP are reported to the OIG. The OIG independently investigates allegations of serious misconduct (criminal or otherwise), fraud, or sensitive matters. When an OIG investigation has identified violations of law, the case is presented to the U.S. Attorney's Office for prosecutorial consideration. If the matter is declined for prosecution, the final investigative report is provided to the BOP for appropriate administrative action.

Allegations of BOP employee misconduct that are not investigated by the OIG are investigated by local BOP investigators at the prisons, with oversight from staff in the Office of Internal Affairs. After allegations have been investigated and the charges validated, an official of the prison reviews the investigative report and proposes an administrative action to impose. A second prison official then reviews the proposal and makes the final determination of administrative action ranging from an oral reprimand up to and including termination.

Hiring Process

Although staff at the BOP's 116 individual prisons handle key steps in the hiring process, the Consolidated Employee Services Center in Grand Prairie, Texas, centralizes most aspects of the hiring process and provides guidance to the prisons on hiring procedures. The Center verifies that each applicant has met the BOP's required minimum qualifications. Below, we briefly discuss the BOP's specific process for selecting and hiring Correctional Officers. Figure 1 at the end of this Background section depicts the basic process new Correctional Officers go through. Appendix IV provides a more detailed discussion.

<u>From Application to Interview</u>

The BOP hires Correctional Officers exclusively at the entry-level pay grades of GL-5 and GL-6.[6] An applicant's previous work experience and education determine at which grade the individual will start. Applicants initiate the hiring process by completing the BOP's online application for the Correctional Officer position through the

---

[5] The OIG's Investigations Division has jurisdiction to investigate all allegations of crimes or misconduct made against Department of Justice employees, including those of the BOP.

[6] Correctional Officers, like many federal law enforcement employees, are on the GL pay scale. The pay range for GL-5 and GL-6 Correctional Officers is $38,619 to $51,193 per year.

USAJOBS.gov job portal. Application questions cover topics that include past work history; education; veterans' preference; and knowledge, skills, and abilities. The BOP's automated system assigns a score according to the applicant's answers. At the time of our analysis, applicants had to score at least 70 out of a possible 110 points to be considered further.[7] The Consolidated Employee Services Center sends lists of qualified applicants to the prisons advertising Correctional Officer positions.

At the prisons, Human Resources Managers conduct credit checks through a national credit reporting company and criminal record checks through the Federal Bureau of Investigation's (FBI) National Crime Information Center (NCIC) before the applicants undergo pre-employment interviews.[8] A Human Resources Manager reviews the results of the credit check prior to the interview.

The pre-employment interview uses a battery of standardized questions to collect information about an applicant's past and current behavior. A Human Resources Manager or designated alternate conducts the interview and records the applicant's responses on a form. The applicant is informed at the beginning of the interview that lying may result in termination or being barred from future federal employment. At the conclusion of the interview, the applicant is asked to sign a statement attesting that their interview responses are accurate and true.

The BOP uses the pre-employment interview information in three ways. First, it compares the information provided by the applicant with 30 measureable thresholds in the BOP's Guidelines of Acceptability to determine whether an applicant is suitable for a Correctional Officer position (discussed below). If applicants exceed any one Guideline threshold, they are considered unsuitable and can only be hired if they receive waivers. Second, it compares the information with applicants' responses to the SF-85PS security form, which asks about drug and alcohol use as well as medical history, and is completed after the applicant receives a conditional offer of employment. Third, it compares

---

[7] In response to the May 11, 2010, Presidential Memorandum, Improving the Federal Recruitment and Hiring Process, the BOP has since changed to a points-based categorical rating system of Best Qualified (90 to 100 points), Highly Qualified (80 to 90 points), and Qualified (70 to 80 points).

[8] The NCIC is an electronic clearinghouse of crime data that can be accessed by virtually every criminal justice agency nationwide. A records check searches NCIC files that include Wanted Persons, the National Sex Offender Registry, Protection Orders, Known or Appropriately Suspected Terrorists, and Immigration Violators. NCIC webpage, http://www.fbi.gov/about-us/cjis/ncic/ncic (accessed June 7, 2011).

the information with the findings of a background investigation conducted later in the process by the Office of Personnel Management (OPM) to determine whether the applicant has been truthful (discussed later in this section).

The BOP's Guidelines of Acceptability cover employment history; military history; financial history; dishonest conduct, excessive use of force, and integrity; and criminal and driving history. Examples of the types of thresholds the Guidelines establish include:

- the number of times fired from employment for cause or disciplined within a set number of years and

- the amount of past due debt where satisfactory arrangements for a payment schedule have not been made.[9]

An applicant found suitable as a result of the pre-employment interview is advanced to the panel interview.

From Interview to Conditional Offer

The panel interview evaluates an applicant's qualifications, knowledge, and skills necessary for the position. In addition, the panel considers intangible factors such as character, integrity, decision making ability, and judgment in assessing the suitability of applicants. Interviewers also may follow up on issues covered in the pre-employment interview.

Panel interviews are conducted by three prison staff members trained to conduct the interviews: a human resources employee, a Correctional Services supervisor or manager (such as a Lieutenant or a Captain), and a psychologist or similarly qualified staff member. Before an interview begins, panel members review all available applicant information.

Panel members note both the strengths and weaknesses of an applicant's answers on a standardized rating form. They also rate the candidate in 10 job-related areas using a rating scale of "Excellent," "Acceptable," or "Unacceptable." If a panel member rates an applicant "Unacceptable" in any area, the panel member must document the

---

[9] The BOP considers the specific thresholds to be sensitive and restricts access to their contents so that potential applicants cannot circumvent the thresholds. Consequently, in this public report, we do not disclose the specific thresholds.

reason. After the interview, the three panel members' ratings are combined, and the panel determines whether the applicant is acceptable. If the panel members disagree, the Human Resources Manager reaches a decision according to the ratings of the majority of the panel.

Applicants who reach this point must undergo a National Agency Check (NAC), which consists of searches of national security databases and fingerprint files. If some results of the NAC are delayed, the BOP may make its hiring decision based on the fingerprint check alone. Following successful NAC or fingerprint screening, applicants may receive a conditional offer of employment and start working on a probationary status. New hires remain on probationary status for a period of 1 year after their entry-on-duty date.

From Conditional Offer to Permanent Employment

A conditional offer of employment allows Correctional Officers to begin work only if they receive satisfactory results from a physical examination, urinalysis for detection of illegal drugs, and any self-reported mental health history.

Every newly hired Correctional Officer must also undergo a background investigation. The background investigation process is initiated after the BOP makes a conditional offer of employment that is accepted by the applicant. The investigation is conducted by OPM on behalf of the BOP and covers facets of an individual's past that may provide insight into the individual's reliability, trustworthiness, loyalty to the United States, and conduct and character.[10] To initiate the investigation process, newly hired Correctional Officers are required to submit details of their background in the Questionnaire for Public Trust Positions, including past home addresses, family information, and travel history.

While OPM begins the investigation process as soon as a newly hired Correctional Officer has been given a date to report to work, the

---

[10] The BOP used limited background investigations for Correctional Officers during the time period of our review, but has since switched to full background investigations. Limited background investigations include written inquiries covering the most recent 3 years, record searches covering 5 years, and a credit search covering 7 years. Results of the credit search are provided to the requesting agency only if OPM identifies a potential credit problem. Full background investigations extend the written inquiries to cover 5 years. Additionally, OPM provides the requesting agency with the results of the credit search whether there is a potential credit problem or not.

investigation is completed after the employee has begun work. It may take several months to over a year to complete an investigation.[11] When OPM completes a background investigation, it assigns a case closing code. A case closing code is determined based on the presence or absence of and severity of potential character and conduct concerns within an individual's background investigation, weighted in light of the passage of time.

Although applicants generally are hired before their background investigations are conducted, they will be asked to explain in writing any discrepancies found between their pre-employment interview responses and what was discovered during the background investigations. An employee may be terminated if found to have been dishonest during the application process.[12]

Background Investigation Adjudication

Once OPM completes the background investigation, the BOP's Security and Background Investigation Section (SBIS) adjudicates any discrepancies that have arisen in the individual's background information. Although OPM raises any derogatory issues it has discovered when performing an investigation, SBIS conducts its own evaluation of the investigation's results and may or may not conclude that an issue raised by OPM is of concern. Similarly, SBIS may deem an issue not raised by OPM as a negative factor.

If SBIS finds a discrepancy between information found in the background investigation and what the applicant told the BOP during the pre-employment interview, and such information would have barred the person from being hired under the Guidelines of Acceptability, it will, in writing, formally ask the employee questions relating to the topic. These questions are known as interrogatories. Answers to these interrogatories determine whether a Correctional Officer will be retained or terminated. In rare cases, the Correctional Officer's Warden may

---

[11] In FY 2009, the most recent year for which data is available, OPM took an average of 3.5 months to complete Correctional Officer background investigations.

[12] Until 2006, prison staff checked applicants' references with prior employers, extending back 5 years, to verify the employment information and work history applicants provided during their pre-employment interviews. The BOP discontinued the practice in February 2006 because OPM verifies employment information during its background investigation process. We are assessing the reference checking practices of Department components, including the BOP, in a separate review.

request a waiver of the Guidelines of Acceptability. Such a waiver must be supported by the BOP Regional Director.

In its section on "Objecting to an Eligible," OPM's *Delegated Examining Operations Handbook* states that various factors, including intangible ones such as personal characteristics, can be considered when determining suitability of applicants. The Handbook states that a selecting official may object to an applicant for reasons such as education, experience, false statements, past performance ratings, inability to obtain a security clearance, personal characteristics, habitual use of alcohol, illegal use of narcotics, or for medical reasons. The selecting official must ensure that the reason for the objection is proper and adequate, and does not violate merit system principles.[13]

---

[13] OPM, *Delegated Examining Operations Handbook: A Guide for Federal Agency Examining Offices* (May 2007), 159-161.

Figure 1: Fundamental Steps of the Correctional Officer Hiring Process through the End of the Probationary Year

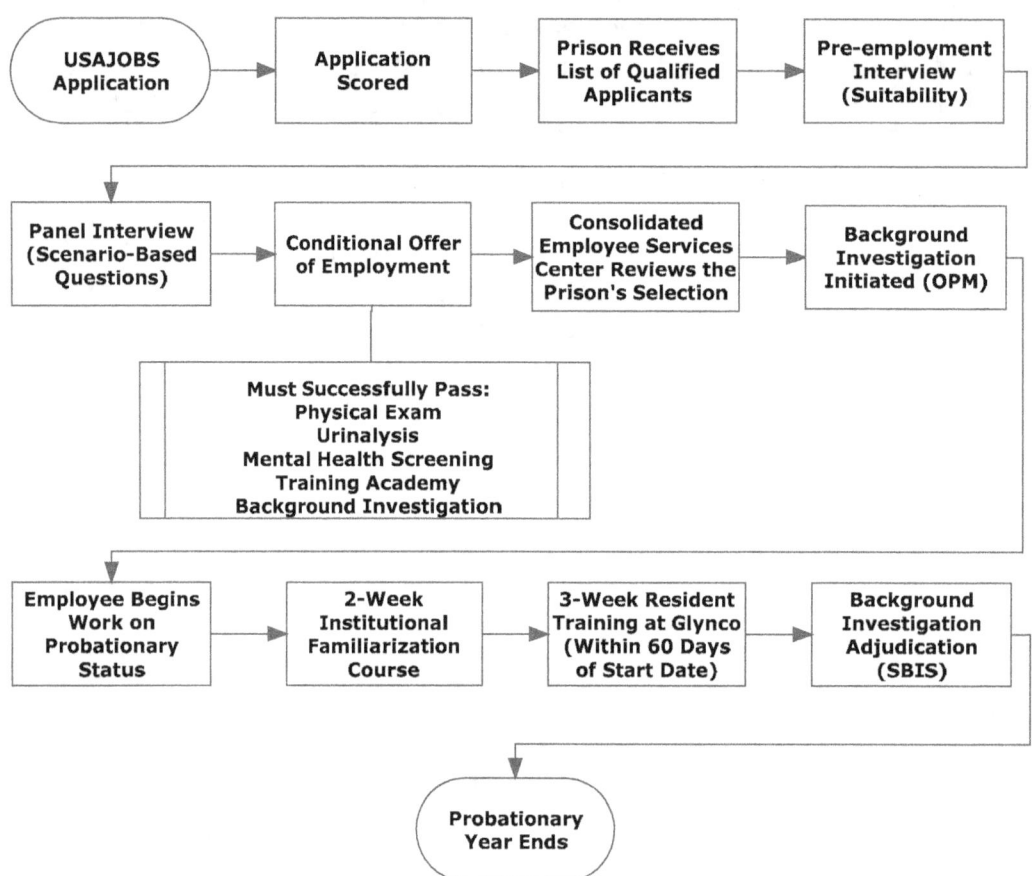

SCOPE AND METHODOLOGY OF THE OIG REVIEW

Scope

We reviewed the BOP's process for hiring Correctional Officers at its prisons nationwide. We examined how the BOP assesses the qualifications and suitability of applicants, beginning with the application process and ending with the BOP's final adjudication of background investigations. We did not review the hiring processes at the privately managed or community-based facilities and local jails the BOP uses under contract to house approximately 18 percent of its inmates.[14]

We analyzed BOP Correctional Officer misconduct and arrest data for the 10-year period from FY 2001 through FY 2010 to identify trends involving newly hired Correctional Officers. We compared those trends with misconduct and arrest trends for all BOP Correctional Officers and BOP staff in general. We also analyzed data provided by the BOP's Security and Background Investigation Section to evaluate whether, from FY 2007 through FY 2010, the BOP adjudicated Correctional Officer background investigations within the officers' 12-month probationary periods.

We analyzed background information for approximately 12 percent of the 3,731 Correctional Officers that were hired by the BOP during FY 2007 and FY 2008 to identify any characteristics that predicted future conduct.[15] Our analysis included all BOP Correctional Officers who had committed substantiated misconduct and received discipline of at least a 1-day suspension or who had been arrested during their first 2 years after being hired. For comparison purposes, we analyzed the background information of a sample of Correctional Officers hired in that time period who had good conduct records for the first 2 years of their service with the BOP.[16]

We focused the scope of our review on Correctional Officer conduct in their first 2 years of service with the BOP. For Correctional Officers

---

[14] BOP website, http://www.bop.gov/about/index.jsp (accessed June 8, 2011).

[15] We extracted 175 different elements of information from each of the 458 background investigation files (a total of approximately 78,300 data elements).

[16] We defined "good conduct" as not having been the subject of any misconduct allegation or arrests in their first 2 years of service with the BOP.

---

hired in FY 2007 and FY 2008, we were able to analyze their conduct records for a full 2 years after the entry-on-duty date, through September 30, 2010. We could not analyze employee records for Correctional Officers hired before FY 2007 because the BOP maintains certain records for only 2 years.

Methodology

The review employed a multi-disciplined approach consisting of evaluation of hiring policies, interviews, site visits, and statistical procedures including classification tree and logistic regression analyses.[17] A detailed description of our methodology and regression analysis is in Appendices I, II, and III.

---

[17] Classification tree and logistic regression analysis are statistical techniques used to find relationships between variables for the purpose of predicting values.

> **Misconduct allegations and arrests of BOP Correctional Officers have increased in the last decade, with both being most likely to occur during the early years of Correctional Officers' service. Our classification tree and logistic regression analyses showed that combinations of characteristics in applicants' backgrounds are predictive of bad behavior, but the BOP's hiring process does not have a systematic method of evaluating combinations. Finally, we found that the BOP has reduced the possibility of permanently hiring unsuitable Correctional Officers by shortening the amount of time taken to adjudicate background investigations.**

Misconduct allegations and arrests of BOP Correctional Officers have increased in the last decade.

Misconduct Allegations

A total of 39,555 misconduct allegations against Correctional Officers were reported to the BOP's Office of Internal Affairs between FY 2001 and FY 2010. The number of allegations reported doubled from FY 2001 to FY 2010, with most of the increase coming during the first half of the decade. The BOP's Office of Internal Affairs opened investigations into 2,299 misconduct allegations against Correctional Officers in FY 2001, and 4,603 allegations in FY 2010.

Allegations against Correctional Officers rose faster than the increase in the number of Correctional Officers. The number of allegations made against Correctional Officers increased 107 percent from FY 2001 through FY 2007, even though the number of Correctional Officers employed by the BOP increased only 17 percent during this time.[18] Since FY 2007, when allegations against Correctional Officers

---

[18] An FY 2003 BOP policy change may have contributed to the relatively higher number of misconduct allegations reported in FY 2003 through FY 2010 as compared with FY 2001 and FY 2002. Specifically, in FY 2003 BOP prisons were instructed to report all allegations of misconduct to the BOP's Central Office. The policy in place in FY 2001 and FY 2002 did not mandate the reporting of all allegations and, according to the BOP, not all allegations were reported.

were at their highest, the BOP has seen a decline of 3.5 percent, from 4,770 allegations in FY 2007 to 4,603 in FY 2010, even as the number of Correctional Officers employed by the BOP increased 6 percent (see Figure 2).[19] Despite the decline in misconduct allegations against Correctional Officers in FY 2008 and 2009, both the number of allegations and the rate of allegations per 1,000 Correctional Officers were much higher in FY 2010 than they had been in FY 2001.

Figure 2: Misconduct Allegations Made Against Correctional Officers, FY 2001 through FY 2010

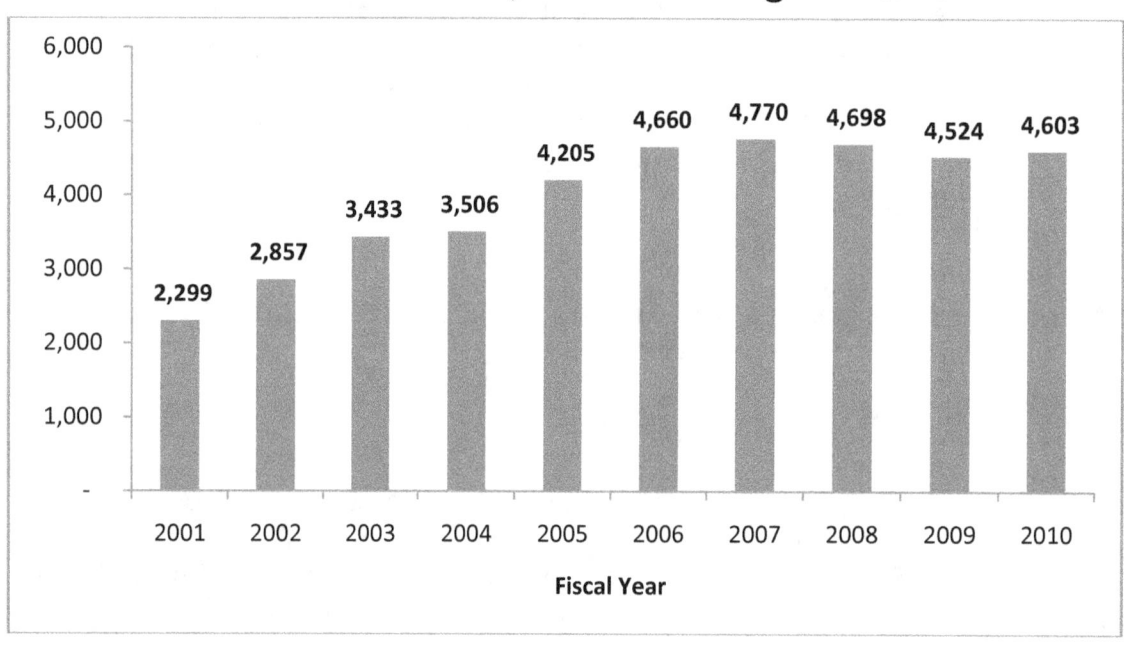

Source: BOP Office of Internal Affairs data.

Correctional Officers were investigated for misconduct disproportionately to their representation in the BOP workforce throughout the decade. Correctional Officers accounted for approximately 40 percent of BOP staff, but were the subject of 53 percent of the misconduct allegations made in FY 2001 and 63 percent of the allegations made in FY 2010 (see Table 1).

---

[19] The number of allegations made per 1,000 Correctional Officers dropped 9 percent over this time, from 315 allegations per 1,000 in FY 2007 to 288 allegations per 1,000 in FY 2010.

Table 1: Percentage of BOP Staff Who Are Correctional Officers Compared with Percentage of Misconduct Allegations Against Correctional Officers, FY 2001 through FY 2010

Fiscal Year	Percentage of BOP Staff Who Are COs	Percentage of Misconduct Allegations Made Against COs
2001	38%	53%
2002	38%	56%
2003	39%	56%
2004	39%	56%
2005	41%	58%
2006	41%	58%
2007	42%	59%
2008	42%	62%
2009	42%	62%
2010	42%	63%
Average	**40%**	**58%**

Source: BOP Office of Internal Affairs data.

Of the 32,455 misconduct allegations made against Correctional Officers between FY 2001 and FY 2009 for which there was a final resolution, 16,717 (52 percent) were substantiated.[20] While this percentage held relatively stable for allegations reported between FY 2001 and FY 2008, the percentage of allegations made in FY 2009 that were substantiated dropped to 43 percent. Table 2 shows the percentage of allegations made each year that were substantiated.

---

[20] We could not determine what percentage of misconduct allegations made in FY 2010 were substantiated because at the time the BOP provided us the data, investigations into 67 percent of the misconduct allegations made in FY 2010 were still open.

**Table 2: Number and Percentage of Allegations
Made Against Correctional Officers
that Were Substantiated, FY 2001 through FY 2009**

Fiscal Year	Number of Allegations with Final Resolution	Number of Allegations Substantiated	Percentage of Allegations Substantiated
2001	2,273	1,188	52%
2002	2,823	1,475	52%
2003	3,384	1,827	54%
2004	3,470	1,868	54%
2005	4,162	2,180	52%
2006	4,544	2,448	54%
2007	4,499	2,295	51%
2008	4,022	2,044	51%
2009	3,278	1,392	43%
Overall	**32,455**	**16,717**	**52%**

Note: The number of allegations with a final resolution is less than the total number of allegations made each year because some allegations did not have a final resolution recorded in the BOP's database because they were still open. We excluded these allegations before calculating the percentage of allegations substantiated.

Source: BOP Office of Internal Affairs data.

Arrests

Arrests of Correctional Officers as a result of substantiated allegations involving criminal activity have also increased since FY 2001. From FY 2001 through FY 2010, the OIG Investigations Division reported that a total of 272 Correctional Officers were arrested. During this period, Correctional Officer arrests rose from 18 in FY 2001 to 34 in FY 2010, an increase of 89 percent (see Figure 3). There was only a 24-percent rise in Correctional Officer staffing levels at the BOP during the same time period.

While there is no single explanation for the increase in Correctional Officer arrests from FY 2001 to FY 2010, during the course of our review BOP officials suggested two factors likely to have contributed to the rise. First, in 2004 the BOP implemented a near-total ban on lighted tobacco products in its prisons, which had the effect of turning cigarettes into contraband. Second, recent years have seen stricter enforcement of prohibitions against inappropriate sexual relationships in prison due to heightened awareness and federal legislation.[21]

Figure 3: Total BOP Correctional Officer Arrests, FY 2001 through FY 2010

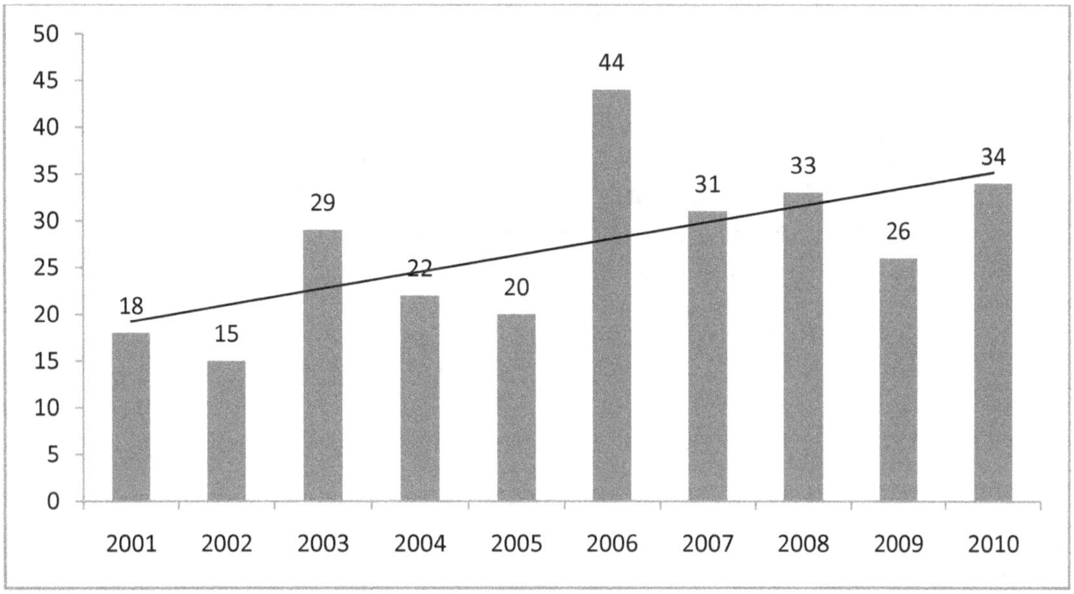

Source: OIG Investigations Division data.

Misconduct allegations and arrests are most common in Correctional Officers' early years.

Misconduct

Over half (58 percent) of the Correctional Officers who had substantiated allegations of misconduct, and who received discipline of at least a 1-day suspension between FY 2001 and FY 2009, were disciplined for conduct that occurred within their first 2 years of service with the BOP. We analyzed data provided by the BOP's Office of Internal

---

[21] The *Prison Rape Elimination Act of 2003* called on the Department of Justice to make the prevention of prison rape a top priority; the *Violence Against Women and Department of Justice Reauthorization Act of 2005* increased the penalty for certain sexual abuse crimes and made those crimes felonies instead of misdemeanors; and the *Adam Walsh Child Safety and Protection Act of 2006* further increased the maximum penalties for certain sexual abuse crimes and requires federal employees who are found guilty of any sexual abuse offense involving a federal prisoner to register as sex offenders.

Affairs to calculate the amount of time from an employee's first day of employment to the date that the employee became the subject of a misconduct investigation. We identified 1,020 Correctional Officers that were hired and that had substantiated misconduct allegations that resulted in serious discipline.[22] Of the 1,020 Correctional Officers that received serious discipline, 587 were disciplined for behavior that occurred within 2 years of their start date.[23]

Arrests

When we analyzed arrest data for FY 2001 through FY 2010, we found that, of the 272 Correctional Officers arrested between FY 2001 and FY 2010, over one-quarter (27 percent) were arrested for behavior that took place during their first 2 years of service (see Figure 4).

---

[22] We identified 5,345 substantiated misconduct allegations against Correctional Officers hired between FY 2001 and FY 2009, and counted the number of unique Social Security Numbers associated with each misconduct record to determine the number of Correctional Officers involved in those allegations. We defined "serious discipline" as suspension, reassignment, demotion, resignation under inquiry, retirement under inquiry, termination, or a combination of these penalties.

[23] The severity of punishment administered to BOP Correctional Officers for work-related misconduct, as federal workers, is in part determined by the employee's past work record, including length of service, performance on the job, ability to get along with others, and dependability.

Figure 4: Year of BOP Service at Time of Incident Leading to Arrest, FY 2001 through FY 2010

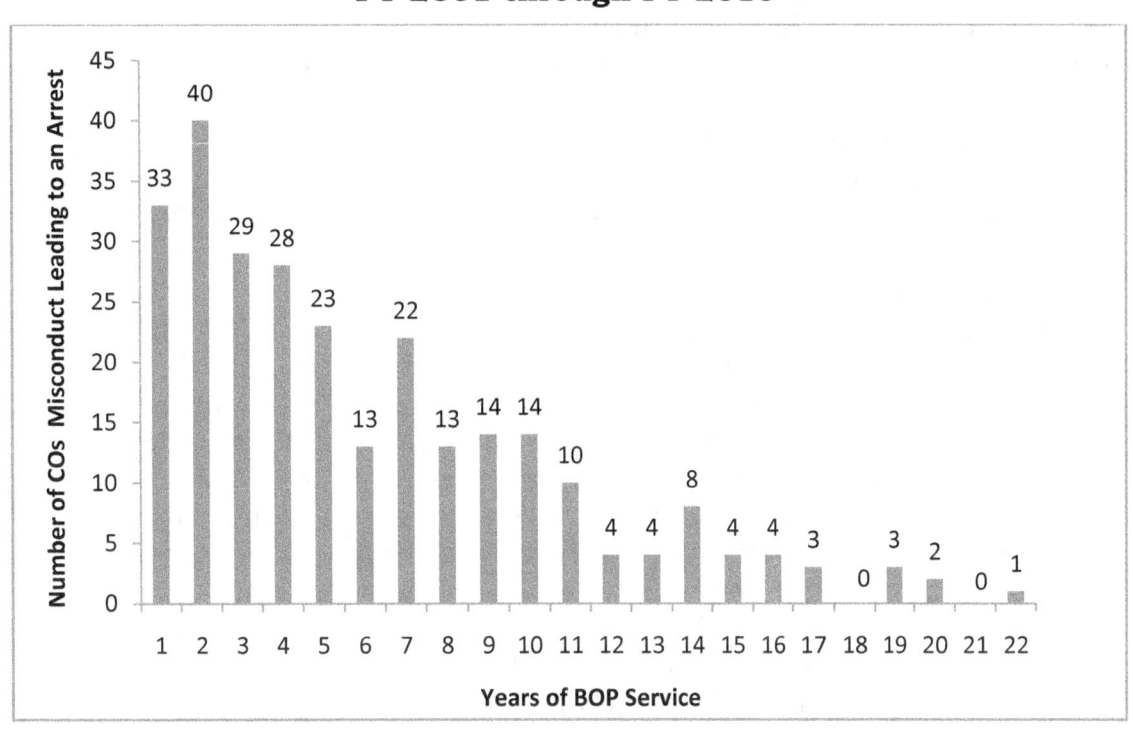

Source: OIG Investigations Division.

Because of the extent to which Correctional Officers committed misconduct during their first 2 years, we examined the characteristics of those officers to determine whether characteristics or patterns discernable at hiring could predict future misconduct.

Classification tree and logistic regression analyses show combinations of applicants' background characteristics are predictive of bad behavior, but the BOP's hiring process does not have a systematic method of evaluating combinations.

Extensive classification tree, conditional inference tree, and logistic regression analyses conducted by the OIG found that combinations of certain applicant characteristics have strong relationships with an increased likelihood of substantiated misconduct resulting in at least a 1-day suspension during the first 2 years after a Correctional Officer begins work. To conduct the analyses, we identified all 171 of the 3,731 Correctional Officers hired in FY 2007 and FY 2008 who had substantiated misconduct within 2 years after being hired and who received discipline of at least a 1-day suspension. We then selected a random sample of 287 Correctional Officers hired in FY 2007 and FY 2008 with no reported misconduct. Our analyses of data from the personnel files of those 458 Correctional Officers found 2 characteristics that, standing alone, were predictive of good behavior, and 7 characteristics that, when they appeared in particular combinations, were predictive of bad behavior. Appendix III provides a detailed discussion of our methodology and analysis.

The proof of concept demonstrated by our statistical procedures and logistic regression analysis found that combinations of applicants' characteristics are predictive of future conduct. We believe the BOP should assess the value of establishing a composite scoring system that takes into account combinations of characteristics for evaluating Correctional Officer applicants' suitability as part of its hiring process. Below, we summarize the results of our analyses and outline the concept that combinations of background characteristics are a useful indicator of future behavior.

Predictors of Correctional Officer Behavior

Of the 175 Correctional Officer characteristics we analyzed, 2 were predictive of a greater likelihood of good behavior. Seven other characteristics, if they appeared in particular combinations, were predictive of a higher likelihood that Correctional Officers would commit substantiated misconduct resulting in at least a 1-day suspension within the first 2 years of being hired.

The two characteristics that were predictive of good conduct were duration of the longest civilian job previously held and education level. Specifically, as the duration of Correctional Officers' longest held prior civilian jobs increased, the likelihood they would commit misconduct while employed by the BOP decreased. Similarly, Correctional Officers who had earned college credits or a degree had a significantly lower likelihood of committing substantiated misconduct resulting in at least a 1-day suspension within the first 2 years of being hired. The BOP does not currently require a specific level of education for Correctional Officer applicants unless they lack qualifying work experience. While we are not providing an education recommendation, we believe the BOP should consider the predictive relationship established by our analysis between good conduct and officers with at least some college-level education when determining goals for the desired makeup of the BOP's Correctional Officer workforce.

The characteristics that were predictive of bad conduct were being disciplined at past jobs, separating from past jobs under unfavorable circumstances, having one or fewer jobs with supervisory responsibilities, having past due debts, having relatives who are inmates, using marijuana, and working for less than 9.8 years at longest-held civilian job.[24] However, these characteristics, which we will discuss further below, were predictive only when they appeared in particular combinations. Although these particular combinations predicted bad conduct, they included characteristics that would otherwise be viewed by most people as good (such as having no past due debts). Bad conduct was more likely to result if an applicant's background information displayed one of the three combinations of characteristics in Table 3.[25]

---

[24] Because our study examined a wide range of information available to the BOP, not all of the exact data points included in the combinations we identified could be used by the BOP in making hiring decisions. For example, the vast majority (95 percent) of Correctional Officers in our sample met the criteria of having held their longest civilian job for less than 9.8 years. Consequently, it would be impractical for the BOP to limit its hiring to only candidates with prior experience exceeding 9.8 years (although the BOP would be able to favorably consider longer periods of employment, generally). Similarly, although the BOP uses information on incarcerated relatives when assigning Correctional Officers to facilities, having a confined relative is not a reason for the BOP to reject an otherwise qualified Correctional Officer candidate. Although the BOP could not use these specific characteristics in making hiring decisions, we included them because they demonstrate the proof of concept that combinations of information available to the BOP can be used to better focus hiring decisions.

[25] The statistical confidence of this finding is .98. In other words, there is only about a 1 in 50 chance this was a random occurrence.

Table 3: Combinations of Characteristics that Make Bad Conduct More Likely Within 2 Years of Correctional Officers' Hiring

Characteristic	Combination 1	Combination 2	Combination 3
Separated from past job under unfavorable conditions	—	No	Yes, once or twice
Disciplined at past job	Yes	—	—
Supervisory experience	—	Fewer than 2 positions	—
Relatives who are inmates in any federal, state, or local institution	—	No	—
All credit accounts current	Yes	No	No
Past use of marijuana	Yes	—	—
Worked for less than 9.8 years at longest-held civilian job	Yes	Yes	Yes

Note: A dash means the characteristic was not part of the combination.

Five of the seven characteristics are self-explanatory, but two require explanation:

- Prior Unfavorable Job Separation – Refers to applicants leaving past jobs under unfavorable circumstances other than being dismissed for cause.[26] The BOP asks applicants if they were dismissed or if they resigned in lieu of dismissal from a job, but not whether other unfavorable circumstances occurred at the time they left a previous job. Such circumstances include leaving without giving notice, being involved in a fight with a co-worker, or not being eligible for rehire because of behavior problems such as temperament or an inability to get along with others. When we factored these other types of unfavorable circumstances into our analyses we found that, if certain other characteristics were also present in a Correctional Officer's background, they were predictive of substantiated misconduct resulting in at least a 1-day suspension within the first 2 years of being hired by the BOP.

---

[26] We did not find any correlation between the number of times an officer had been dismissed for cause from past jobs and an officer's behavior after joining the BOP. Therefore, our analysis focused on unfavorable job separations other than dismissal for cause.

- <u>All Credit Accounts Current</u> – Refers to applicants' credit history. In the table above, "no" means applicants with at least one collection account with a balance or at least one financial judgment or at least one account with a past due balance. "Yes" means applicants with no such balances or judgments.

While the combinations our analyses identified are statistically significant, some are not intuitive. For example, Combination 1 identifies "all credit accounts current," a seemingly positive aspect of an individual's background, to be a variable that when taken in combination with three other variables is predictive of bad behavior. What our analysis shows is that combinations of characteristics matter in predicting the likelihood of misconduct resulting in at least a 1-day suspension. If the BOP were to systematically evaluate individuals based on combinations of factors in addition to the single thresholds on which it now relies, it might enhance its screening practices. The combinations the BOP uses would likely not be identical to ours. Instead, if the BOP assesses the value of using combinations in its screening practices and decides to implement a composite scoring system, the system would likely include the BOP's own analysis and judgment and could be used in conjunction with or incorporated into the Guidelines of Acceptability.

As discussed in the Background section, OPM assigns a case closing code according to a process that assesses the severity of potential character and conduct concerns found during the course of the background investigation. The Chief of the BOP's SBIS told us he often sees that OPM has assigned a more serious case closing code because of the presence of several less serious issues in different categories covered in an investigation. He said that if the BOP had a similar capability, it might be able to screen out unsuitable candidates earlier in the process. According to the Chief of SBIS, composite scoring would enable staff to consistently rate the composite picture of candidates, would align the BOP's rating methodology more closely with OPM's, and would therefore result in less uncertainty about whether objections to candidates will be sustained.

Currently, BOP hiring officials are given discretion to subjectively evaluate the composite picture of an individual's background, in addition to the objective thresholds described in the Background section of our report, in order to determine suitability. However, in practice, few hiring managers use this ability due to uncertainty about whether an objection to a candidate based on a manager's discretion will be sustained by the Consolidated Employee Services Center. We believe such uncertainty could be alleviated by

---

Combined Versus Individual Characteristics

Below is a real example from the BOP's files of how a Correctional Officer applicant's background characteristics, when looked at individually, may not exceed the Guidelines of Acceptability, but taken in combination with each other may reflect a background not suitable for work in a correctional setting.

A Correctional Officer hired by the BOP had the following negative characteristics:

- Resigned from two previous jobs in correctional facilities under unfavorable circumstances. This person quit both jobs in the middle of work shifts, with one resignation taking place immediately preceding a meeting with supervisors to address allegations of introducing contraband into the prison.

- Terminated from one previous job.

- A Protection from Abuse Order was filed against this person after allegedly assaulting a significant other with a tire iron.

- Showed anger and hostility while working with juvenile inmates at a previous correctional job.

- History of absences without leave at previous jobs.

- Several financial accounts in collections.

- At least one default judgment related to personal finances.

This person was hired by the BOP because none of the individual behaviors exhibited above exceeded the Guidelines of Acceptability. After entering on duty at a BOP prison, this individual received two substantiated incidents of misconduct and resigned while still on probation.

creating a composite scoring system that is used consistently across the BOP. Indeed, the Consolidated Employee Services Center would then have a specific guideline it could point to in order to sustain an objection. As is the case with applicants who exceed any one Guideline of Acceptability threshold, a failure to pass the composite scoring system could be overcome with a waiver.

The results of our regression analysis show proof of the concept that combinations of background characteristics are predictive of future conduct and can be used to decrease the chances of hiring an individual who will later commit misconduct. Creating a composite scoring mechanism could strengthen the BOP's ability to reject an unsuitable applicant before an offer of employment is made and strengthen SBIS's ability to judge an employee's overall suitability once the background investigation is complete.

Potential Benefits of Composite Scoring

To provide an estimate of the benefits of a composite scoring mechanism, we performed an additional analysis to find how many of the Correctional Officers in our sample would have been identified by the three predictive combinations that surfaced in our analyses. This was an analysis based on the findings of the classification tree, conditional inference tree, and logistic regression analyses, but performed separately. We found that, based on our sample, the tangible benefits of the BOP using composite scoring to assess Correctional Officer applicants could be substantial. Specifically, the 3 predictive combinations would have identified 67 (39 percent) out of 171 Correctional Officers in our sample who committed serious, substantiated misconduct. In contrast, the 3 predictive combinations would have identified only 32 (11 percent) out of 287 Correctional Officers who did not commit misconduct.[27] Thus, the combinations would have been a useful tool in assessing Correctional Officer applicants in our sample and, consequently, would have enhanced the safety and security of the prisons in which the 67 identified Correctional Officers were hired.[28]

---

[27] Any screening factors, including those currently found in the BOP's Guidelines of Acceptability, eliminate some applicants who will never commit misconduct along with applicants who will.

[28] Because the population of Correctional Officers we drew our sample from did not include the applicants who had already been screened out by the BOP's Guidelines

(Cont'd.)

Our additional analysis also found that the BOP could realize cost savings by using composite scoring to identify Correctional Officers who are more likely than others to commit misconduct. Correctional Officers that are terminated due to misconduct or resign during misconduct inquiries force the BOP to expend resources hiring and training replacement officers. Taken together, the 3 combinations detailed above would have identified 41 Correctional Officers in our sample who were terminated due to misconduct or resigned during misconduct inquiries. Had the BOP not hired those officers, it would have represented a cost savings to the BOP for items such as training, overtime paid to staff covering shifts of the departed Correctional Officers, additional hours of administrative work by BOP support staff, OPM background investigations, equipment and uniforms, and drug screening.

The BOP's Ability to Use Predictive Characteristics

If the BOP were to develop a composite scoring system, it might need to alter the manner in which it collects personal information, depending on the characteristics it includes. While the data we used in our regression analysis came from the BOP's files, we pulled some key data from portions of records that do not now factor into a hiring decision or that are not available to the BOP when it makes a hiring decision. Below are the characteristics we found to be predictive individually or in combination with one another, and a description of where we obtained the information for each one within the BOP's files.[29]

---

of Acceptability, it was not possible to estimate the additional number of applicants from that population who would have met the criteria of one or more of the combinations.

[29] We previously noted that the vast majority (95 percent) of Correctional Officers in our sample met the criteria of having held their longest civilian job for less than 9.8 years and that it would be impractical for the BOP to limit its hiring to only candidates with prior experience exceeding 9.8 years in length (although the BOP would be able to favorably consider longer periods of employment, generally). Similarly, although BOP uses information on incarcerated relatives when assigning Correctional Officers to facilities, having a confined relative is not a reason for the BOP to reject an otherwise qualified Correctional Officer candidate. We included these characteristics in our analysis because they demonstrate the proof of concept that combinations of information available to the BOP can be used to better focus managers' hiring decisions.

- Education Level – We obtained the data on college education from the background investigation files the BOP receives from OPM after Correctional Officers have already begun work.[30]

- Duration of Prior Civilian Job – We used the OPM background investigations to determine the number of months Correctional Officers had been employed at their prior civilian jobs.

- Prior Job Discipline – We used applicants' responses during pre-employment interviews and OPM background investigations to determine whether Correctional Officers had been disciplined at past jobs.

- Prior Unfavorable Job Separation – We obtained information about prior unfavorable job separations from the OPM background investigations.

- Past Supervisory Experience – We extracted our data on past supervisory experience from the OPM background investigations, which include applicants' descriptions of their former jobs. We also read OPM-administered interviews of former co-workers and supervisors who mentioned applicants' former supervisory experience.

- All Credit Accounts Current – We obtained financial history data from the single credit report BOP prisons request as part of pre-employment screening or from the OPM background investigations, which contain a consolidated report from all three of the national credit reporting bureaus.

- Relatives Who Are Inmates – We used the information about relatives of applicants confined in federal, state, or local facilities that the BOP obtains during pre-employment interviews.

- Use of Marijuana – We obtained the information about marijuana use from the pre-employment interviews.

---

[30] We collected information about education levels from the background investigations because the BOP's human resources database had inaccurate education information for about 50 percent of the Correctional Officers in our sample.

Conclusion

The BOP's system for evaluating applicants' backgrounds does not include a mechanism for systematically considering combinations of characteristics to derive a risk factor when deciding whether to hire or make a Correctional Officer a permanent member of the BOP's staff. However, the BOP has the authority to establish such a system. The proof of concept demonstrated by our statistical procedures and logistic regression analysis found that combinations of applicants' characteristics are predictive of future conduct. We believe the BOP should assess the value of establishing a composite scoring system for evaluating Correctional Officer applicant suitability.

The BOP reduced the possibility of permanently hiring unsuitable Correctional Officers by shortening the amount of time taken to adjudicate background investigations.

Ensuring the timely adjudication of background investigations is essential because if derogatory information is uncovered during the employees' probationary period, it is easier for the BOP to terminate them. Once employees complete their probationary periods, they have the full bargaining unit appeal rights of permanent employees. As stated by the Merit Systems Protection Board, probationary "terminations typically have not given rise to the same level of uncertainty and additional administrative costs that accompany the removals of employees who are entitled to full procedural and appeal rights."[31]

We found the BOP greatly reduced the length of time it took to complete background investigations of Correctional Officers from FY 2007 through FY 2010. Because Correctional Officers remain on probationary status for 1 year, we focused our analysis on the number of background investigations that took over 1 year to complete. We found the percentage of Correctional Officer background investigations completed after the probationary year ended decreased from 43 percent and 44 percent in FY 2007 and FY 2008, respectively, to 14 percent in FY 2009 and 6 percent in FY 2010 (see Figure 5).

---

[31] Merit Systems Protection Board, *Navigating the Probationary Period After Van Wersch and McCormick* (September 2006), i.

Figure 5: Percentage of Correctional Officer Background Investigations Completed After the Probationary Period Ended, FY 2007 through FY 2010

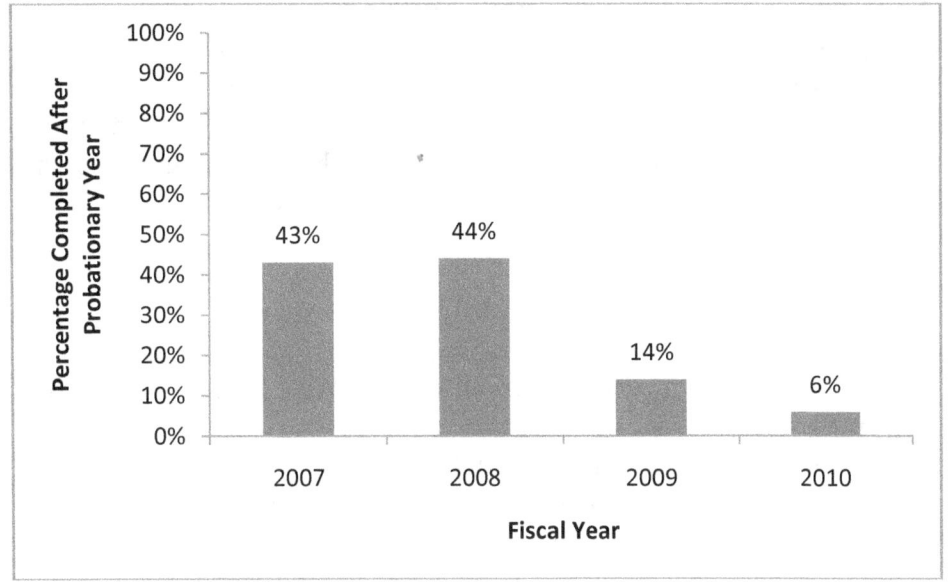

Source: BOP SBIS data.

The BOP official in charge of background investigation adjudication attributed the decrease to three primary reasons. First, OPM decreased the amount of time it took to conduct background investigations. Second, the BOP decreased the amount of time it took to adjudicate the completed investigations by adding 6 positions to the SBIS staff in January 2009, bringing the total number of employees to 32. Third, SBIS developed a system that identifies employees who have been employed at least 10 months and whose background investigations have not been adjudicated. SBIS then assigns a specially designated team in an effort to complete the adjudications before the employees' 12-month probationary periods end.

The BOP's improvement in the timely adjudication of background investigations puts it in a stronger position to remove unsuitable Correctional Officers before they become permanent employees.

CONCLUSIONS AND RECOMMENDATION

The BOP's improvement in the timely adjudication of background investigations has put it in a stronger position to remove unsuitable Correctional Officers before they become permanent employees. In FY 2010, the BOP completed 94 percent of Correctional Officer background investigations within the 12-month probationary period, up from 43 percent in FY 2007, making it less likely that the BOP will permanently hire unsuitable officers.

To further reduce the likelihood of Correctional Officer misconduct and arrests, particularly during the first 2 years of being hired, the BOP could consider additional ways of assessing applicants. Currently, the BOP does not include a method of considering or assigning weights to combinations of characteristics to derive a risk factor in its assessment process. However, the BOP has the authority to establish such a method.

The OIG's analyses of a sample of Correctional Officers hired in FY 2007 and FY 2008 found that the tangible benefits of the BOP using composite scoring to assess Correctional Officer applicants could be substantial. Taken together, the 3 predictive combinations that surfaced in our analyses would have identified 67 (39 percent) out of 171 Correctional Officers in our sample who committed substantiated misconduct resulting in at least a 1-day suspension. In contrast, the combinations would have screened out only 32 (11 percent) out of 287 Correctional Officers who did not commit misconduct. Thus, the combinations would have been a useful tool in assessing Correctional Officer applicants in our sample and, consequently, would have helped to protect the safety and security of the prisons in which the 67 identified Correctional Officers worked.

In addition to helping keep BOP prisons safe, using composite scoring could also realize cost savings. Correctional Officers who are terminated due to misconduct or who resign during misconduct inquiries force the BOP to expend resources hiring and training replacement officers. Taken together, the 3 combinations detailed above would have identified 41 Correctional Officers in our sample who were terminated due to misconduct or resigned during misconduct inquiries. Had the BOP not hired those officers, it would have represented a cost savings to the BOP for items such as training, overtime paid to staff covering shifts of the departed Correctional Officers, additional hours of administrative work by BOP support staff, OPM background investigations, equipment and uniforms, and drug screening.

To reduce the potential for hiring unsuitable Correction Officers and thereby to reduce misconduct among Correctional Officers, we recommend that the BOP:

1. Consider developing a composite scoring mechanism for assessing the suitability of Correctional Officer applicants.

APPENDIX I: OIG METHODOLOGY FOR THIS REVIEW

The review employed a multi-disciplined approach consisting of evaluation of hiring policies, regression analysis, and site visits. We visited the BOP's headquarters in Washington, D.C.; the Consolidated Employee Services Center in Grand Prairie, Texas; the Security and Background Investigation Section in Dallas, Texas; the Federal Correctional Complex at Tucson, Arizona; the United States Penitentiary at Hazleton, West Virginia; and the Federal Law Enforcement Training Center in Glynco, Georgia.

Regression Analysis

Our data analysis proceeded in a detailed, phased approach to identify the variables that were statistically most closely related to committing misconduct and in constructing a final overall explanatory model. The data available for analysis contained 458 cases and 175 variables.

Misconduct Files: We reviewed the BOP's misconduct database to identify all 171 of the 3,731 Correctional Officers hired during FY 2007 and FY 2008 who committed misconduct during their first 2 years of service (ending September 30, 2010), which resulted in a punishment of at least a 1-day suspension up to and including termination.[32] We used the date that the BOP initiated a misconduct investigation as an approximation of the date on which the misconduct was committed.[33]

Good Conduct Files: Using data of the 3,731 Correctional Officers hired between FY 2007 and FY 2008 provided by the BOP, we identified and randomly selected 287 Correctional Officers hired in FY 2007 or FY 2008 who had not been the subject of any misconduct allegations or arrests in their first 2 years of service with the BOP. We excluded from

---

[32] We included in our sample individuals who received penalties of termination, suspension, reassignment, reduction in rank, or who resigned or retired under inquiry, or who received a combination of penalties. We did not include in our sample those with an administrative sanction of less than a 1-day suspension.

[33] Correctional Officers did not have to receive discipline within 2 years of entry on duty to be included in our sample because it takes the BOP a median of 8 months to investigate misconduct allegations. Rather, we sampled Correctional Officers who were disciplined for conduct that occurred within 2 years of entry on duty, even if the officer had been with the BOP for more than 2 years by the time a final disciplinary decision was made.

this good conduct sample any Correctional Officers with:
(1) investigations of misconduct still open, (2) allegations that were substantiated but that resulted in a penalty less severe than a 1-day suspension, or (3) allegations that were investigated but that were not substantiated.[34] We excluded these cases so that our sample would consist of two more divergent groups: those with misconduct who received administrative discipline resulting in at least a 1-day suspension or were arrested, and those without misconduct who were not investigated for misconduct at all.

Variables: As proof of the concept that combinations of applicant background information could be used to better focus the BOP's Correctional Officer hiring decisions, we examined a very wide range of applicant background characteristics that would be available to BOP personnel managers and hiring officials during the hiring process.[35] We collected data on each of the 458 Correctional Officers in our sample from the following files and sources: background information collected by the BOP before it made its hiring decisions, forms completed by applicants to initiate an OPM background investigation, the OPM background investigation reports, and documents generated by the BOP during its adjudications of the OPM background investigations.[36]

---

[34] Penalties that we considered less severe than a 1-day suspension and therefore excluded from our sample were a written reprimand, an oral reprimand, "other," and no action.

[35] Though we considered 175 applicant background characteristics, not all of the data points that emerged in the combinations of characteristics that our analysis identified as being predictive of conduct, would or could be used by the BOP in making hiring decisions. Two such characteristics – duration of (the applicant's) prior civilian job and having relatives who are inmates – would not be considered by the BOP in a hiring decision because of the associated practical or legal limitations of doing so. These limitations are described in the report.

[36] At the time we selected our sample, the BOP retained a copy of the OPM background investigation report for only 1 year after an individual left the agency. For 108 of the 458 files selected for our sample (24 percent), the Correctional Officers had left the BOP more than 1 year before we made our data request; therefore, the BOP could not provide us with copies of these background investigation reports. We obtained archived copies of these reports from OPM. Archived background investigation reports included all of the same documentation as background investigation reports we obtained from the BOP except for copies of credit reports obtained by the BOP before it made its hiring decisions and copies of documents generated by the BOP during its adjudications.

We entered these data into an Access database model in seven broad informational categories: general demographic, personal life, financial, prior civilian employment, military service, criminal and drug history, and driving record information. A list of all variables for which we collected data is in Appendix II.

At the conclusion of data entry, we conducted logic checks as well as frequency checks in order to clean our data. Logic checks were performed to flag data entries whose values were illogical and therefore suspect. Frequency checks were performed in order to look for and correct data field values that evidenced data entry error.

To identify personal background characteristics associated with Correctional Officer misconduct, we used descriptive statistics, correlations, univariate and bivariate analyses, multivariate classification trees, and logistic regression analyses. Univariate and bivariate statistical analyses were used to narrow the 175 variables to a smaller set with the strongest relationships to misconduct. We then employed classification tree logistic regression models to estimate the effects of Correctional Officers' demographic and personal history variables on the likelihood of receiving a substantiated misconduct within the first 2 years of service.[37] Logistic regression analysis is a widely accepted method to examine factors associated with an outcome variable of interest, such as misconduct, controlling for the potential effect of other factors. One of our main reasons for using a multivariate model was to determine whether differences in the likelihood of committing misconduct were accounted for by significant differences in personal demographic and other characteristics that the BOP collects during the Correctional Officer pre-employment screening process.

Phases of Analysis: For the first step, we used univariate analysis to explore the distributions of the variables. Univariate analysis is the examination of a single variable and its characteristics (for example, mean, median). This exercise allowed us to better understand the demographics of our data and identify where recoding or additional verification was needed. Most importantly, this analysis revealed the extent of missing values in each of the variables, which was important for the subsequent stages of analyses. Thirty-two variables that we collected were excluded from the univariate analysis because they had no

---

[37] We use the term "serious substantiated misconduct" to describe a substantiated misconduct allegation that results in an administrative sanction of at least a 1-day suspension up to and including termination.

meaningful information or cannot be considered by the BOP during hiring, such as marital status, gender, race, and number of dependents.

We next analyzed each variable individually against the misconduct/good conduct variable through bivariate analysis. This analysis allowed us to test how well one variable predicted the value of another variable, for our purpose, a person's misconduct status. This activity identified 16 variables with statistically significant (unlikely to have occurred by chance) independent associations with misconduct status. These 16 variables were then selected for inclusion in the logistic regression modeling.

Because committing misconduct is the result of a complex interaction of many factors, we next performed a series of multivariate analyses to identify the relationships among the variables acting together on misconduct status. While the bivariate tests allowed us to identify variables with strong independent associations with misconduct, we then performed a statistical "binary/conditional inference tree" modeling to help us determine combinations and levels of variables that were related to misconduct jointly. From this activity, five interaction terms arose that most closely related with misconduct. Five new variables were then added to our data set. Each Correctional Officer was coded according to whether he or she met the criteria specified by each interaction term.

While the preceding analyses revealed differences in the proportion of Correctional Officers likely to commit substantiated misconduct across background characteristic groups, they did not control for other factors that also might relate to likely misconduct. Therefore, we next employed logistic regression models to predict which factors were associated with committing substantiated misconduct, controlling for other characteristics. Incorporating the 16 selected independent and 5 interaction term variables, we used logistic regression models to estimate the likelihood a Correctional Officer would commit substantiated misconduct. For each of our logistic regression models, we tested various model specifications to assess the model fit and stability of our estimates.[38]

---

[38] Statistical models cannot control for all variables potentially related to misconduct, such as whether an individual had experienced physical abuse as a child. To the extent omitted but relevant variables are correlated with those factors that were incorporated into our models, the estimates are subject to potential bias.

Background Investigations

We reviewed data from the BOP's Security and Background Investigation Section to analyze the timeliness of the BOP's adjudication of OPM background investigations of Correctional Officers hired from FY 2007 through FY 2010.

Misconduct and Arrest Analysis

We reviewed 70,602 allegations of misconduct reported to the BOP's Office of Internal Affairs between FY 2001 and FY 2010 to determine the prevalence of allegations reported against Correctional Officers.[39] Specifically, we determined the number of allegations reported each year, and examined whether the number of allegations reported was commensurate with changes in the population of Correctional Officers. We determined the percentage of allegations reported each year which resulted in substantiated misconduct. We also analyzed data provided by the OIG's Investigations Division for trends in the number of Correctional Officers arrested on criminal charges from FY 2001 through FY 2010.[40]

State Department of Corrections Questionnaire

We sent questionnaires to 18 state departments of corrections to gain insights into Correctional Officer screening and selection approaches in order to compare the BOP with the greater correctional community. We requested information about their hiring and screening procedures, including copies of their specific policies on hiring and background investigations. We also requested statistical data such as numbers of Correctional Officers hired in FY 2007 and FY 2008, and Correctional Officer misconduct and arrest numbers for those 2 years. All 18 states responded to our questionnaire and sent copies of policies. Although some states provided statistical information, we were unable to provide a statistical comparison of misconduct and arrest data across all

---

[39] The BOP's Office of Internal Affairs received a total of 77,466 allegations of misconduct during these 10 years. We excluded 6,864 of these allegations from our analysis because they were reported from contract prisons instead of from BOP-managed prisons. We focused our analysis on the remaining 70,602 allegations.

[40] The OIG's Investigations Division has jurisdiction to investigate all allegations of crimes or non-litigation-related misconduct made against Department of Justice employees, including those of the BOP. The BOP's Office of Internal Affairs does not maintain information on arrests of Correctional Officers.

states and the BOP because some states do not track the data we requested and others cautioned us about the potential inaccuracy of numbers they sent.

Selected results from the questionnaire sent to participants are in Appendix V. The 18 state departments of correction that participated in our survey were:

Alabama	Louisiana	North Carolina
Arizona	Michigan	Ohio
California	Mississippi	Oklahoma
Florida	Missouri	Pennsylvania
Georgia	New Jersey	Texas
Illinois	New York	Virginia

APPENDIX II: VARIABLES COLLECTED DURING FILE REVIEW

We reviewed 458 background investigation files, and collected data on the following 175 variables and sub-variables from each file. As noted elsewhere in this report, we excluded 32 of these variables from our analyses because they had no meaningful information or cannot be considered by the BOP during hiring, such as marital status, gender, race, and number of dependents. Our analyses did not find most of the other 143 variables to be predictive of misconduct resulting in at least a 1-day suspension in a Correctional Officer's first 2 years of BOP employment.

General Demographic Information

1. Name
2. Date of birth
3. Social Security Number
4. Gender
5. Race
6. Date employee filled out the Questionnaire for Public Trust Positions (SF-85P)
7. Date began work at the BOP
8. Prison to which employee is assigned to work
9. Grade level at which employee was hired (GL-5 or GL-6)
10. Number of items marked as a potential issue on OPM's Case Closing Transmittal, the cover sheet that accompanies a completed investigation

Personal Life Information

11. Marital status
    a. For married employees, length of marriage (in years)
    b. For married or separated employees, whether employee and spouse live together
    c. For divorced employees, calendar year in which divorce finalized
12. Number of dependents
13. Number of immediate family members currently in jail (spouse, children, parents, or siblings)
14. Number of extended family members currently in jail (all other relatives)
15. Number of family members employed by the BOP
16. Number of residences within last 7 years
17. Number of years living in current residence

18. Number of years living in current state
19. Whether the employee received treatment for a mental health condition within the last 7 years
20. Number of statements by the employee which we characterized as "honest admissions"

We considered an "honest admission" to be any disclosure of potentially negative information by the employee that would not have been uncovered during the normal course of the background investigation. The most common "honest admission" we saw in these files was an employee's confession of petty shoplifting during childhood. Another common "honest admission" was an employee's confession of taking the occasional pen or notepad from a previous employer.

Financial Information

21. Number of open credit card accounts
    a. Balance owed on those open credit card accounts
22. Number of open mortgage loans
    a. Balance owed on those mortgage loans
23. Number of foreclosures
    a. If foreclosure occurred, calendar year of most recent foreclosure
24. Number of open vehicle loans
    a. Balance owed on those open vehicle loans
25. Number of open other loans (such as student loans or home equity loans)
    a. Balance owed on those other open loans
26. Amount of taxes owed to any federal, state, or local government
27. Number of collection accounts on credit report with a remaining balance
    a. Balance owed on those collection accounts
28. Whether the employee filed for bankruptcy within the last 10 years
    a. If yes, calendar year in which bankruptcy was filed
29. Number of tax liens filed against the employee
    a. If liens filed, calendar year of most recent lien
30. Number of legal judgments listed on employee's credit report
    a. If legal judgments listed, calendar year of most recent judgment
31. Number of evictions for financial reasons
32. Whether employee disclosed any financial obligations that are not listed on the credit report (such as an obligation to pay child support)
33. OIG assessment of whether employee is current with all financial obligations

We considered an employee to be current with all financial obligations if the credit report showed no collection accounts with a remaining balance, and the payment history for all of the open loans (credit cards, mortgages, vehicles, and other loans) showed that no past due balances were owed on those accounts.

Prior Civilian Employment Information

34. Whether the employee had prior federal employment (not counting service in the military)
    a. If the employee had prior federal employment, the highest grade level achieved in that prior employment
35. Whether the employee previously held a security clearance
    a. Whether the employee ever had a security clearance suspended or denied
36. Number of times the employee has been fired as a result of misconduct or poor performance
    a. If the employee has been fired, calendar year of most recent firing
37. Number of times employee was disciplined at work (not including firing)
38. Number of times employee separated from a prior job under unfavorable circumstances (not including firing)
39. Number of jobs held within the last 7 years
40. Duration of the longest-held prior job, in months
41. Number of prior jobs involving supervision of other people

This may include supervision of other employees, such as a manager, or supervision of other individuals who are not fellow employees, such as a teacher.

42. Whether employee has completed any work-related training courses or obtained any training certifications
43. Whether the employee has prior correctional experience
    a. If yes, total number of months of prior correctional experience from one or more jobs
44. Whether the employee has prior civilian law enforcement experience other than in corrections (such as a police officer or a sheriff's deputy)
    a. If yes, total number of months of prior civilian law enforcement experience from one or more jobs

Military Information

45. Whether the employee ever served on active duty in the United States military
46. Whether the employee ever served in the military reserves or the National Guard

We collected the following 11 variables only for those employees who reported active duty service and/or reserve duty service:

47. Highest rank achieved
48. Date of discharge
49. Type of discharge
50. Total length of military service, in months

If the employee reported both active duty service and reserve duty service, we added the number of months spent in each type of military service and recorded the grand total.

51. Number of summary courts martial
    a. If one or more summary courts martial, calendar year of most recent one
52. Number of special courts martial
    a. If one or more special courts martial, calendar year of most recent one
53. Number of general courts martial
    a. If one or more general courts martial, calendar year of most recent one
54. Number of non-judicial punishments (may be called Article 15 or Page 11, depending on branch of service)
    a. If one or more non-judicial punishments, calendar year of most recent one
55. Whether employee was deployed to Iraq or Afghanistan
56. Whether employee had military law enforcement experience
    a. If yes, total number of months of prior military law enforcement experience from one or more jobs
57. Number of military commendations received which indicate a high level of performance

Criminal and Drug History

The following eight variables are based on specific questions that the BOP asks applicants during their pre-employment interviews.

58. Number of times employee took money or merchandise from a previous employer, or from a store
     a.   If one or more incidents, value of money or merchandise taken
     b.   If one or more incidents, calendar year of most recent incident
59. Number of times employee made intentional false statements, or was involved in deception or fraud (including falsification of his or her BOP application)
60. Number of times employee has offered or accepted a bribe
61. Number of times employee has been involved in extortion or coercion
62. Number of times employee has been involved in introducing contraband into a correctional environment
     a.   If one or more incidents, calendar year of most recent introduction of contraband
63. Number of times employee has been involved in excessive use of force as a law enforcement official, conduct such as abuse of any person detained or confined in law enforcement's custody, or aiding and abetting any such acts
     a.   If one or more incidents, calendar year of most recent incident
64. Number of uses of physical force or violence (not including any incidents counted in the variable above)
     a.   If one or more incidents, calendar year of most recent incident
65. Number of occurrences of domestic abuse or child abuse
     a.   If one or more incidents, calendar year of most recent incident

For past criminal behavior, we first counted the number and type of criminal charges that had been filed against the employee in the past, without regard to whether any of these charges resulted in a conviction. We subdivided criminal charges into the following 10 categories. Examples are listed for each category, but those examples are not necessarily an exclusive list of the charges that we counted in that category.

66. Number of violent charges (assault, battery, menacing)
     a.   If one or more charges, calendar year of most recent charge
67. Number of property charges (vandalism, burglary)
     a.   If one or more charges, calendar year of most recent charge
68. Number of monetary charges (embezzlement, writing bad checks)
     a.   If one or more charges, calendar year of most recent charge
69. Number of weapons charges (possessing a firearm without a license)
     a.   If one or more charges, calendar year of most recent charge
70. Number of vehicular charges, excluding driving while intoxicated (reckless driving)
     a.   If one or more charges, calendar year of most recent charge
71. Number of driving while intoxicated charges

a.   If one or more charges, calendar year of most recent charge
72. Number of other alcohol-related charges, excluding driving while intoxicated (minor in possession of alcohol, drunk in public)
    a.   If one or more charges, calendar year of most recent charge
73. Number of marijuana charges (possession)
    a.   If one or more charges, calendar year of most recent charge
74. Number of illegal drug charges, excluding marijuana (possession)
    a.   If one or more charges, calendar year of most recent charge
75. Number of other charges (disorderly conduct, any charges that do not fit into one of the other categories listed)
    a.   If one or more charges, calendar year of most recent charge

After we counted the total number of criminal charges that had been filed against the employee, we counted the number of those charges which resulted in a criminal conviction. We subdivided convictions into the same 10 categories:

76. Number of violent convictions
    a.   If one or more convictions, calendar year of most recent conviction
77. Number of property convictions
    a.   If one or more convictions, calendar year of most recent conviction
78. Number of monetary convictions
    a.   If one or more convictions, calendar year of most recent conviction
79. Number of weapons convictions
    a.   If one or more convictions, calendar year of most recent conviction
80. Number of vehicular convictions
    a.   If one or more convictions, calendar year of most recent conviction
81. Number of driving while intoxicated convictions
    a.   If one or more convictions, calendar year of most recent conviction
82. Number of other alcohol-related convictions
    a.   If one or more convictions, calendar year of most recent conviction
83. Number of marijuana convictions
    a.   If one or more convictions, calendar year of most recent conviction
84. Number of other illegal drug convictions
    a.   If one or more convictions, calendar year of most recent conviction

U.S. Department of Justice   41
Office of the Inspector General
Evaluation and Inspections Division

85. Number of other convictions
    a.   If one or more convictions, calendar year of most recent conviction
86. Whether the employee has ever used marijuana
    a.   If yes, calendar year of last use
87. Whether the employee has ever used an illegal drug other than marijuana
    a.   If yes, calendar year of last use
88. Whether the employee has ever used alcohol while on the job
    a.   If yes, calendar year of last use
89. Whether the employee has ever used illegal drugs (including marijuana) while on the job
    a.   If yes, calendar year of last use
90. Whether the employee has ever come to work while under the influence of any illegal drug (including marijuana)
    a.   If yes, calendar year of last occurrence
91. Whether the employee has ever refused to submit to an employer's drug test
    a.   If yes, calendar year of last refusal
92. Number of times the employee has undergone treatment for substance abuse
    a.   If one or more treatments, calendar year in which employee last received treatment

Driving History

93. Number of traffic tickets as a result of moving violations
    a.   If one or more, calendar year of most recent ticket
94. Number of times driver's license suspended or revoked
    a.   If one or more, calendar year of most recent suspension or revocation

APPENDIX III: REGRESSION ANALYSIS METHODOLOGY

The objective of the analysis was to develop predictive models between substantiated misconduct (hereafter referred to as misconduct) by Correctional Officers at the Federal Bureau of Prisons, and the data describing multiple characteristics of Correctional Officers obtained from their applications, credit history and background investigations. The data available for analysis had 458 cases and 175 variables. Of these 458 cases, 171 were cases of substantiated misconduct, and 287 were cases where there was no misconduct.

We analyzed the data in a phased manner. The analytical phases were: univariate analysis of the predictors to validate the data in the variables, bivariate analysis relating each of the predictors to substantiated misconduct, multivariate tree analysis to uncover interactions among predictor variables and to predict misconduct, and, finally, multivariate logistic regression modeling to predict misconduct.

Univariate Analyses

Univariate examinations of the data revealed that 22 variables were used mainly for record identification or provided no meaningful data for analysis (for example, names and social security numbers), or were completely missing data. Hence these variables were not considered for analysis. The univariate examinations also helped in classifying the remaining 153 variables as being either categorical (or nominal) or quantitative (numeric or ordinal) in nature.

We examined descriptive statistics such as mean, quartiles, median, variance, and standard deviation for each of the numerical (ordinal or interval scaled) predictors. For categorical variables, we examined the frequency distribution of the counts in the categories.

We modified variables related to date of events (for example, date of marriage) to "number of days before a reference date." The reference date chosen was the enter-on-duty date.

Bivariate Analyses

We conducted bivariate analysis to assess the strength of association of each of the predictor variables with the misconduct variable. We employed two different type tests of association:

1. Chi-Square test of Independence, to test the association of each of the categorical variables with the misconduct dependent variable.
2. Test of equality of means of a variable across the two groups, to test the association of each of the numeric (interval or ratio scaled) variables with the misconduct dependent variable.

Chi-Square tests of independence: Let x and y be two categorical variables, with number of categories M and N. If we consider the cross-tabulation of x and y that has M rows, N columns and sample size of n, with the general cell denoted by the pair (i,j), then the Chi-Square statistic is defined as:

$$\text{Chi} - \text{Square} = x^2 = \sum_{i=1}^{M} \sum_{j=1}^{N} \frac{(n_{ij}-e_{ij})^2}{e_{ij}} \qquad (1)$$

Where

- n_i is the number of cases in the ith category of variable x
- n_j is the number of cases in the jth category of variable y, and
- n_{ij} = number of cases in the ith category of variable x and j^{th} category of y.
- e_{ij} is the expected count in the $(i,j)^{th}$ cell and defined as

$$e_{ij} = n_i n_j / n$$

The test statistic given in equation (1) was computed for each of the categorical predictors (independent variables). Each of the categorical predictors were then ranked in an ascending value of probability of the p-value (area under the chi-square distribution to the right of the statistic computed using formula (1)). Lower p-values denoted a more statistically significant association of that predictor with the misconduct dependent variable. We used a p-values of .05 or below to choose variables. We selected six variables based on the p-values.

Tests of Equality of Means across two groups:

Let

- x be a numeric (interval or ratio scaled) predictor variable.
- 1 and 2 denote the two categories – "misconduct" and "no misconduct" of the dependent variable.
- n_1 denote the number of cases in the 1st category (misconduct) of the dependent variable

- n_2 is the number of cases in the 2nd category (no misconduct) of the dependent variable,
- X_1 denote the mean of variable x for the cases that fall in the 1st category of the misconduct dependent variable,
- X_2 denote the mean of variable x for the cases that fall in the 2nd category of the misconduct dependent variable
- Let s_1 denote the sample variance of x for the 1st category of the misconduct dependent variable.
- Let s_2 denote the sample variance of x for the 2nd category of the misconduct dependent variable.

The t statistic to test whether the population means are different is calculated as follows:

$$t = \frac{\bar{X}_1 - \bar{X}_2}{s_{\bar{X}_1 - \bar{X}_2}} \tag{2}$$

Where

$$s_{\bar{X}_1 - \bar{X}_2} = \sqrt{\frac{s_1^2}{n_1} + \frac{s_2^2}{n_2}}$$

s_1^2 and s_2^2 are unbiased estimators of the variance in the two misconduct groups in the sample. The degrees of freedom (d.f.) are calculated as:

$$\text{d. f.} = \frac{\left(s_1^2/n_1 + s_2^2/n_2 \right)^2}{\left(s_1^2/n_1 \right)^2 \big/ (n_1 - 1) + \left(s_2^2/n_2 \right)^2 \big/ (n_2 - 1)}$$

The test statistic (equation 2) was computed for each of the numeric predictors (independent variables). Then, a p-value was determined from the Student's t distribution, and each of the numerical predictors were then ranked in an ascending p-value (area under the tails of the t- distribution) to determine the numeric predictors that have the highest association with the misconduct dependent variable.

Predictors with the lowest p-value have the highest degree of association with the misconduct dependent variable. We selected 11 variables that had p-values below .05 for further consideration in multivariate analysis.

Multivariate Analyses Using Binary Classification Tree Models:

We used two Tree-based analytical modeling approaches to determine the significant combinations of various variables (interactions) that predicted the presence or absence of misconduct:

1. Recursive Partitioning, implemented as "rpart" function in R, and
2. Conditional Inference Trees (implemented as "ctree" in R).

Both Recursive Partitioning and Conditional Inference Trees represent heuristic approaches to predictive modeling that capture non-linearity in the data. While many such approaches exist, we will present one version of the tree algorithm in very generic terms, closely related to the two models that we used, recognizing that there is no one approach that can claim superiority over other approaches.

<u>A General Description of a Binary Classification Tree Modeling Algorithm</u>

Let
- N be the number of cases
- K_c be the number of categorical (ordered or unordered) predictor variables, and K_n be the number of numeric predictors, where $K = K_c + K_n$.
- **y** denote the (N x 1) vector of the binary dependent variable values y_j, , j = 1, ..., N. Permissible values are 1 (Misconduct) and 0 (no misconduct)
- **x_i** denote the vector of values for the ith variable, i = I ... K. Each vector has N values.

Various algorithms have been implemented for Tree modeling. We present below a very generic form of one such algorithm for readers to get a flavor of the analytics used in Tree models.

Tree modeling algorithms can be characterized as repetitive procedures that build trees in the following iterative fashion:

Initial settings: let i = 0, node = 0;

1. i = i + 1
2. Choose variable i

3. If the variable i is a categorical variable, perform the following steps:
   a. If variable i is a categorical variable, count the number of categories (C_i).
   b. Form a 2-way 2x2 cross-tabulation of the dependent variable (**y**) with variable i (**x_i**).
   c. Compute a measure of association using the 2-way cross-tabulation. Call the measure A_i.
   d. Rep*eat the b-c for all possible 2x2 cross-tabulations that can be formed with the C_i categories.
   e. Choose the cross-tabulation that yields the maximum association as the winning cross-tabulation, and record the combinations of levels of variable i that formed the 2 "levels" of the winning cross-tabulation.
4. If the variable i is a numeric variable, perform the following steps:
   a. Choose a "splitting" point in the range of variable x_i. and bin it into two buckets: to the left of it (lower than the chosen point), and right of it (higher than the chosen point).
   b. Form a 2-way 2x2 cross-tabulation of the dependent variable with the new binned variable.
   c. Compute a measure of association using the 2-way cross-tabulation. Call the measure A_i.
   d. Repeat the b-c for different splitting-points until a value is found in the range of variable x_i that maximizes the measure of association A_i.
   e. Choose the cross-tabulation that yields the maximum association as the winning cross-tabulation, and record the "Splitting point" of the winning cross-tabulation.

5. Repeat steps 1-4 for i = 1, ..., K.
6. Choose the variable that has the best association with the dependent variable. Call it the winning predictor, x_w.
7. Divide the cases into the 2 groups specified by variable x_w, and call the nodes n+1 and n+2.
8. Set i = 0.
9. Set n = n+2.
10. Repeat the steps 1-9 for each terminal node found in Step 7.
11. Stop when the node size is less than a pre-specified amount, or the measure of association with dependent variable is not strong enough.

The algorithm detailed above assumes that at every stage of the tree building process, the algorithm compares the "optimal splits for each variable" before choosing which variable to split on. This gets computationally complex and time/resource intensive, especially when one is dealing with many categorical predictors and/or categorical predictors with a large number of categories.

Some current versions of tree models separate out stages of "determining which variable to split on" from "determining the best split for the variable" in two distinct phases.

Rpart in R uses "Gini index" as a measure of association, while ctree in R uses p-values based on statistical tests to determine which variables to split on.

The Gini index is defined as

$$\text{Gini index} = \sum_{i=1}^{L} \sum_{j \neq i, j=1}^{L} p_i p_j$$

where L is the number of categories of the dependent variable, where p_i is the proportion of cases in category i of the dependent variable.

Results of Binary Recursive Partitioning Procedures:

We employed rpart algorithm from R for one of the two binary classification tree analyses. We generated and examined multiple binary trees for their predictions and associated combinations of variables. An eight node classification tree with minimum split size of 60 or more was considered. This option correctly classified 253 out of 287 (over 88 percent) good conducts and 66 of 171 (over 38 percent) of misconducts yielding overall correct classification of 319 of 458 (over 69 percent) as presented in Table 4.

Table 4: Results for 60 Node Tree: Rpart

From Data:	Good conduct	Misconduct	Total from Data
Good conduct	**253 (88.2%)**	34	287
Misconduct	105	**66 (38.6%)**	171
Total from Predictions	302	156	458

The graph of the tree is presented in Figure 6.

Figure 6: Binary Classification Tree

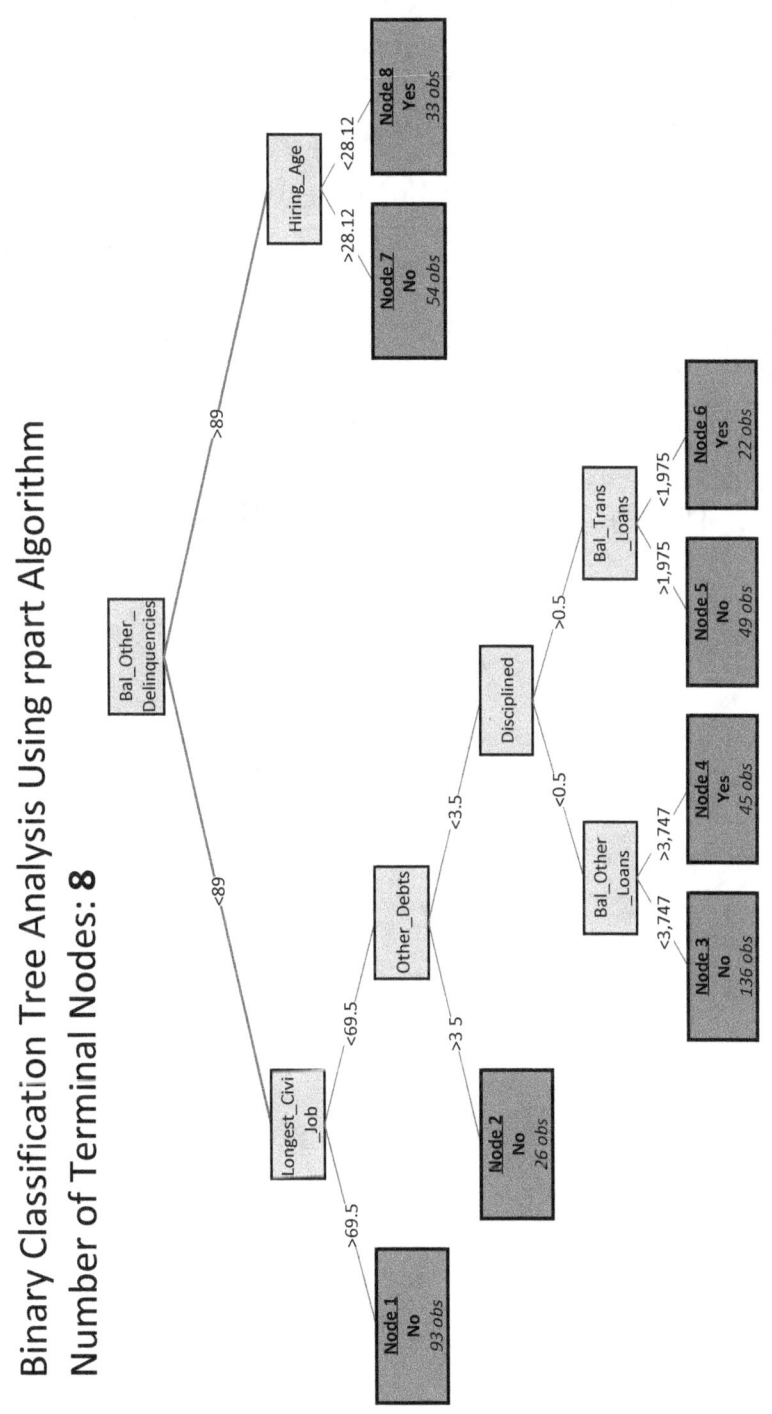

Binary Classification Tree Analysis Using rpart Algorithm
Number of Terminal Nodes: **8**

We employed conditional inference (CI) tree algorithm from R, as in the case of rpart, but with weighting the misconduct case by 2:1 in order to extract the effect of explanatory variables on the response variable. The CI tree analysis resulted with a thirteen terminal node tree as presented below. The correct classification of misconducts was 126 of 171 (over 73 percent) and good conducts 191 of 287 (over 66 percent), as presented in Table 5.

Table 5: Predictions from ctree

	Good Conduct	Misconduct	Total from Data
Good conduct	**191 (66.6%)**	96	287
Misconduct	45	**126 (73.7%)**	171
Total from Predictions	236	222	458

This CI tree graph is also presented in Figure 7.

Figure 7: Binary Classification Tree Analysis

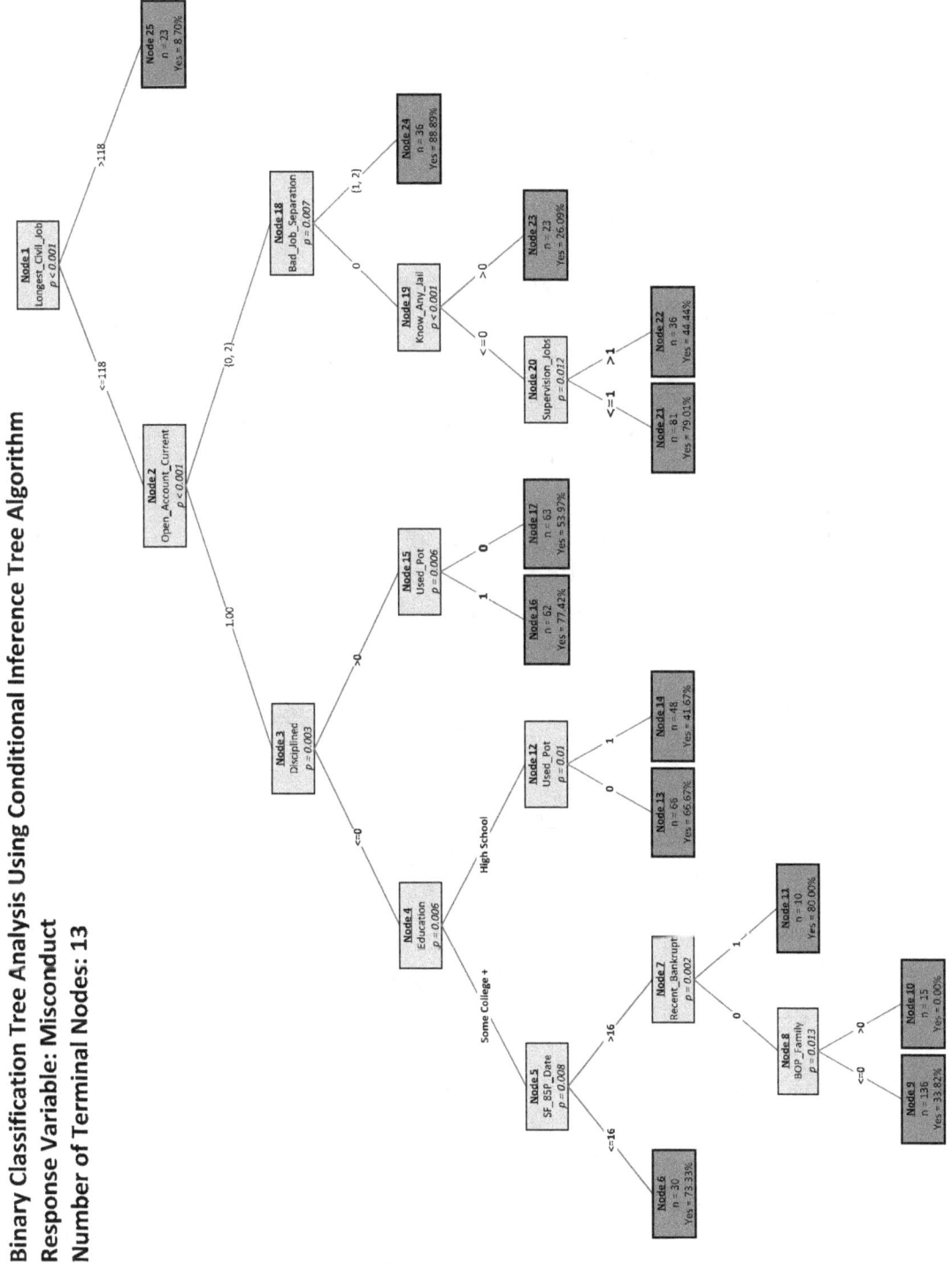

Binary Classification Tree Analysis Using Conditional Inference Tree Algorithm
Response Variable: Misconduct
Number of Terminal Nodes: 13

Multivariate Analysis Using Logistic Regression

Let

- N be the number of cases.
- K+1 be the number of predictor variables, including the additive constant.
- **y** denote the (N x 1) vector of the binary dependent variable values y_j, , j = 1, ..., N. Permissible values are 1 (Misconduct) and 0 (no misconduct).
- $\mathbf{x}_i$ denote the vector of values for the ith case, i = 1 ... N. Each vector $\mathbf{x}_i$ has (K+1) elements x_{ij}, j = 1, 2, ..., K+1.
- **X** denote the N x K+1 matrix of predictors, containing no missing data.
- **β** denote the (k+1 x 1) vector of coefficients for the K variables and an additive constant **β₀.** The elements of **β** are β_0, β_1, β_2,..., β_k, the parameters to be estimated.
- p_i denote the probability that y_i for case i takes on the value "Misconduct". Then probability of "no misconduct" = 1- p_i. Since p_i + (1-p_i) = 1, it can be seen that probability("Misconduct") + probability("no misconduct") = 1, for i = 1, ..., N.

Then, the Logistic Regression equation can be written as

$$\log\left[\frac{p_i}{1 - p_i}\right] = \beta_0 + \beta_1 x_{i1} + \beta_2 x_{i2} + \beta_3 x_{i3} + \dots + + \beta_k x_{ik} \quad (3)$$

The function $\log[p/(1-p)]$ is the "Logit" function. The equation in 3 can be rearranged to get:

$$\text{Probability } (y_i = \text{``Misconduct''}) = p_i = \frac{e^{\beta x_i}}{1+e^{\beta x_i}} \quad (4)$$

Where p_i + (1-p_i) = 1 for 1 = 1,2, ..., N.

In equation (4), the vector of coefficients β is unknown. The most common estimation procedure is the usage of Maximum Likelihood Estimation (MLE) techniques. The likelihood function to be maximized is written as:

$$L = \prod_{i=1}^{N} \left(\frac{e^{\beta x_i}}{1 + e^{\beta x_i}}\right)^{y_i} \left(\frac{1}{1 + e^{\beta x_i}}\right)^{1-y_i} \tag{5}$$

Since the logarithmic transformation increases monotonically, maximizing L is equivalent to Maximizing Log(L), with the additional advantage of obtaining a numerically simpler function. Applying the logarithmic transformation yields:

$$Log(L) = \sum_{i=1}^{N} \log\left\{\left(\frac{e^{\beta x_i}}{1 + e^{\beta x_i}}\right)^{y_i} \left(\frac{1}{1 + e^{\beta x_i}}\right)^{1-y_i}\right\} \tag{6}$$

This function has been shown to be globally concave, and results in globally optimal solutions upon maximization with respect to the unknown parameters in vector β.

To obtain the estimates for β – called $\hat{\beta}$, we need to find the values that maximize the Log(L) function of equation (6). In order to accomplish that, we need to differentiate Log(L) by each of the K+1 coefficients.

The resulting equations after first order differentiation with respect to the coefficients are given as

$$\sum_{i=1}^{N} [y_i - p_i] = 0 \tag{7}$$

when differentiated with respect to the additive constant β_0 , and

$$\sum_{i=1}^{N} x_{ij}[y_i - p_i] = 0 \tag{8}$$

when differentiated with respect to $\beta_1, \beta_2, ..., \beta_k$.

The solution to these equations yields the globally optimal solution. Function glm in R and procedure Logistic Regression in SPSS to find the optimal solutions.

The variance and covariance of the estimated coefficients are based on the theory of maximum likelihood estimation. These estimates are obtained from the second partial derivatives of the log likelihood function specified in equation (6). These second order partial derivatives are:

$$\frac{\partial^2 L(\beta)}{\partial \beta_j^2} = \sum_{i=1}^{N} x_{ij}^2 \, p_i (1 - p_i) \qquad (9)$$

and

$$\frac{\partial^2 L(\beta)}{\partial \beta_j \, \partial \beta_u} = \sum_{i=1}^{N} x_{ij} x_{iu} p_i (1 - p_i) \qquad (10)$$

for $j, u = 1, 2, \ldots, K$.

If we define $\mathbf{I}(\beta)$ as a (K+1) x (K+1) matrix containing the negative of terms defined in equations (9) and (10), then this matrix is called the **information matrix**. The variances and covariances of the estimated coefficients are obtained from the inverse of the information matrix.

Let us denote the inverse of the information matrix as $\mathbf{C}(\beta)$. In the general form, it is not possible to analytically write the expressions for the elements in $\mathbf{C}(\beta)$. The ith diagonal element provides the variance of β_i and the $(i,j)^{th}$ element of this matrix provides the covariance between (β_i, β_j). The standard errors of the estimates are defined as square roots of the ith diagonal of $\mathbf{C}(\beta)$. These standard errors are used in testing the significance of each of the parameters that are estimated in the model.

In order to assess the fit of the logistic regression model, one uses the Akaike Information Criterion (AIC). Though Likelihood ratio based tests, which have a Chi-Square distribution, are typically used to assess model fit, information theoretic criteria such as AIC offer a stricter test for models to pass before they become acceptable.

The model with the lowest AIC score is chosen as the best fitting model. AIC is defined as:

$$\text{AIC} = -2 * \text{Log}(L) + 2 * \text{Number of parameters} \qquad (11)$$

We used AIC as our criterion for selecting the best fitting logistic regression model.

Once the models are estimated, the predicted probability of Misconduct is obtained from equation (4), using the estimated coefficient vector $\hat{\beta}$.

Logistic Regression Analysis Results

To minimize partially missing data problems and to drop redundant and other collinear variables we built multiple binary logit models on the same data set, using 25 variables. In order to select effective interactions (or combinations) of variables, we incorporated the results of classification trees as described above. From the classification tree analysis results, we incorporated two interactions variables from rpart algorithm results and thirteen interactions variables from conditional inference tree algorithm results.

We chose a final model that has minimized Akaike Information Criterion (AIC) and dropped the least number of observations due to missing data. The results of the final logistic regression model analysis are provided in Table 6 below, which contains 10 variables of which 5 are combination variables derived from recursive binary tree analysis.

Table 6: Results of Logistic Regression Analysis

Better Fitting Logistic Regression Model

Variable	Estimate	Std. Error	z value	Pr(>|z|)	
(Intercept)	-0.81	0.44	-1.82	0.0683	.
Education: Some College +	-0.52	0.25	-2.11	0.0351	*
Open_Account_Current =1	0.36	0.39	0.93	0.3534	
Open_Account_Current=2	14.07	882.74	0.02	0.9873	
Longest_Civil_Job	-0.01	0.00	-2.40	0.0163	*
License_Suspended	0.24	0.16	1.52	0.1287	
ctree.n16: Longest Civil Job <= 118 Months Open Account Current = 1 Disciplined > 0 Used Pot: 1	1.33	0.44	3.00	0.0027	**
ctree.n21 Longest Civil Job <= 118 Months Open Account Current : 0 or 2 Number of Bad Job Separations: 0 Know Any Jail = 0 Supervision Jobs <= 1	1.71	0.47	3.66	0.0003	***
ctree.n24: Longest Civil Job <= 118 Months Open Account Current : 0 or 2 Num. of Bad Job Separations:1 or 2	2.57	0.69	3.75	0.0002	***
rpart.n23: Balance Other Delinquencies < 89 Longest Civil Job < 69.5 Other Debts < 3.5 Disciplined >= 0.5 Bal_Trans_Loans < $1,975	0.58	0.35	1.67	0.0958	.
rpart.n7: Balance Other Delinquencies >=89 Hiring Age < 28.12	1.23	0.53	2.31	0.0207	*

Signif. codes: 0 '***' 0.001 '**' 0.01 '*' 0.05 '.' 0.1 ' '

To assess the utility of the final model, we used the model's results to compute a predicted likelihood of misconduct for each of the correctional officers in our sample.[41] After sorting the likelihoods in decreasing order, we calculated the number of actual misconducts in each 10 percent group. The exercise indicates how well the model predicts actual misconducts and whether it might be useful in real world applications.[42]

The table below shows the performance of the logistic regression model in the top 20 percent of those predicted to commit misconduct and the bottom 20 percent, representing those expected to be least likely to commit an early misconduct. We would expect very good predictions of misconduct in the top 20 percent, and a very good prediction of good conduct in the bottom 20 percent. As illustrated in Table 7 below, the model does a good job predicting those most likely to commit misconduct and those most likely to have good conduct histories. Of the 100 correctional officers in our sample predicted to be mostly likely to commit misconduct, 70 of them had a substantiated misconduct allegation. Of the 100 officers predicted to be least likely to have a substantiated misconduct, 84 had no misconduct allegations.

Table 7: Predictions of Misconduct and Good Conduct

Correct Predictions of Misconduct

	Prediction of Top 10%	Prediction of Top 20%	Prediction of Top 100
% Model Prediction	77.5%	67.5%	70.0%

Correct Predictions of Good Conduct

	Prediction of Bottom 10%	Prediction of Bottom 20%	Prediction of Bottom 100
% Model Prediction	92.5%	77.5%	84.0%

---

[41] The final model was based on 395 observations. For 63 of the 458 cases, probabilities could not be computed as data on at least one of the predictor variables was missing.

[42] Ideally, the hold out sample would have been used to test the predictive power of the model. Due to the relatively small size of our sample, setting aside a hold out group was not possible.

The model is more successful in predicting good conduct, but also does well in targeting misconduct, which is expected to be the result of complex factors.

APPENDIX IV: THE BOP'S HIRING AND SELECTION PROCESS

The basic process a new Correctional Officer goes through is described below.

Online Application Process and Scoring

Applicants initiate the hiring process by completing the BOP's online application for the Correctional Officer position through the USAJOBS.gov job portal. Application questions cover topics that include past work history; education; veterans' preference; and knowledge, skills, and abilities. Once completed, the application is scored by the BOP's automated system according to the applicant's answers. The minimum qualifying score is 70 out of a maximum 110 possible points. Scores are used to organize the applicant pool to give the highest scoring applicants the first opportunities for interviews.

Financial History and NCIC Check

Human Resources Managers at individual BOP prisons conduct a credit check through a national credit reporting company and a criminal record check through the FBI's National Crime Information Center on each Correctional Officer applicant prior to the scheduled pre-employment interview. The results of the credit check are reviewed prior to the interview.

The NCIC is an electronic clearinghouse of crime data that can be accessed by virtually every criminal justice agency nationwide. It operates under shared management between the FBI and federal, state, local, and tribal criminal justice agencies. NCIC files that are searched in a record check include Wanted Persons, the National Sex Offender Registry, Protection Orders, Known or Appropriately Suspected Terrorists, and Immigration Violators.[43]

Pre-Employment Interview and Guidelines of Acceptability

Each prison's Human Resources Manager or designated alternate interviews Correctional Officer applicants to screen for derogatory background information as defined in the BOP's Guidelines of

---

[43] FBI website, http://www.fbi.gov/about-us/cjis/ncic/ncic (accessed July 13, 2011).

Acceptability. All BOP employees conducting pre-employment interviews are trained to ask a series of standardized questions about applicants' past and current behavior and note responses on pre-employment interview forms.

Prior to a pre-employment interview, the BOP requires each applicant to be completely truthful. Candidates are informed that if they lie in their pre-employment interview, it may result in termination or debarment from future federal employment.[44] Candidates are asked to sign a statement at the conclusion of their interviews stating that the interview findings are accurate and true. Applicants' responses to pre-employment interview questions are not verified until OPM conducts a background investigation after an individual begins work at the BOP. OPM and the BOP later compare the responses on the forms with the findings of background investigations.

The Guidelines of Acceptability establish over 30 measureable threshold standards covering employment history; military history; financial history; dishonest conduct, excessive use of force, and integrity; and criminal and driving history. The Guidelines are based on the suitability standards established in OPM's Suitability Processing Handbook and the Code of Federal Regulations, and are tailored to work performed in a correctional setting. The BOP considers the specific thresholds of these Guidelines to be sensitive and allows only selecting officials and human resources staff to know what they are. The types of thresholds the Guidelines of Acceptability establish include:

- allowable number of misdemeanor convictions within a set number of years,

- allowable number of times fired from employment for cause or disciplined within a set number of years,

- allowable number of instances of use of physical force within a set number of years,

- allowable past due debt where satisfactory arrangements for a payment schedule have not been made, and

- for applicants who served in the military, allowable number of military judicial and non-judicial punishments within a set number of years.

---

[44] Debarment is a prohibition from taking a competitive service examination or from being hired (or retained in) a covered position for a specific time period.

An applicant who exceeds any one threshold is considered unsuitable and disqualified from the applicant pool. Only if the hiring official recognizes extenuating circumstances, and a Regional Director or Assistant Director grants a waiver, may an applicant exceed Guidelines of Acceptability standards and still be hired.

A candidate found suitable as a result of the pre-employment interview is advanced to the panel interview.

Panel Interview

According to BOP policy, the purpose of the panel interview is to evaluate an applicant's qualifications, knowledge, and skills necessary for the position. In contrast to the pre-employment interview, the panel interview is not meant to delve into the applicant's personal history to judge suitability for employment in a sensitive position. However, interviewers may broach issues covered in the pre-employment interview in the form of follow-up questions. Areas to be evaluated during the panel interview include knowledge, skills, and, abilities needed for the position; general correctional work abilities; and writing skill.

Panel interviews are conducted by three BOP staff members: a human resources employee, a Correctional Services supervisor or manager (such as a Lieutenant or a Captain), and a psychologist or similarly qualified staff member. All interviewers must attend a panel interview course before participating in panel interviews. Before an interview begins, panel members review all available applicant information, such as the pre-employment interview results and application form.

The panel interview process begins with an evaluation of the applicant's writing skills. The applicant is shown a videotape of a work scenario and is asked to write a mock report based on it. Panel members next begin the question and answer portion of the interview by asking follow-up questions they may have about the information the applicant provided in the pre-employment interview and application form. The applicants are then asked standardized questions about work situations to elicit information about their knowledge, skills, and abilities related to the position as well as to correctional work in general.[45] Interviewers are allowed to ask questions other than the standardized questions when

---

[45] The BOP is working with OPM to develop an additional screening tool that includes situational work questions designed to elicit information on the BOP's core values of correctional excellence, respect, and integrity.

necessary to judge the acceptability of an applicant for work in a correctional setting. However, panel members must focus on job-related topics.

Panel members note both the strengths and weaknesses of an applicant's answers on a standardized rating form. They also rate the candidate in 10 job-related areas using a rating scale of "Excellent," "Acceptable," or "Unacceptable." If a panel member rates an applicant "Unacceptable" in any area, the panel member must document the reason. After the interview, the three panel members' ratings are combined, and the panel determines whether the applicant is acceptable. If the panel members disagree, the Human Resources Manager reaches a decision according to the ratings of the majority of the panel.

National Agency Check and Fingerprint Check

Applicants who reach this point must undergo a National Agency Check, which consists of searches of OPM's Security/Suitability Investigations Index, the Defense Clearance and Investigations Index, the FBI Identification Division's name and fingerprint files, and other files or indices when necessary.[46] If some results of the National Agency Check are delayed, the BOP may make its hiring decision based on the fingerprint check alone. Following successful NAC or fingerprint screening, applicants may receive a conditional offer of employment and have their first day of work scheduled.

Physical and Mental Health Screening

Conditional offers of employment are contingent upon applicants receiving satisfactory results from a physical examination, urinalysis for detection of illegal drugs, and self-reported mental health history.

During the mental health history screening, applicants must disclose whether they have consulted with a mental health professional (such as a psychiatrist, psychologist, or counselor) or another health care provider about a mental health-related condition in the last 7 years. Applicants answering yes to this question must provide dates of treatment as well as the name and address of the provider they saw.

---

[46] The OPM Security/Suitability Investigations Index is a database of investigations previously conducted by OPM. The Defense Clearance Investigation Index is a database of investigations previously conducted by the Department of Defense. The FBI Name Check is a check of all FBI investigative and administrative cases to see if the individual's name is associated with any of those cases.

Applicants do not have to answer in the affirmative if they were involved only in marital, grief, or family counseling not related to violence.

Background Investigation

Every newly hired Correctional Officer must undergo a background investigation and is subject to reinvestigation every 5 years during BOP employment. The background investigation process is initiated once the BOP makes a conditional offer of employment that is accepted by the applicant. The investigation is conducted by OPM on behalf of the BOP and covers facets of an individual's past that may give insight into the individual's reliability, trustworthiness, loyalty to the United States, and conduct and character.[47] To initiate the investigation process, newly hired Correctional Officers are required to submit details of their background in the Questionnaire for Public Trust Positions, including past home addresses, family information, and travel history.

While OPM begins the investigation process as soon as a newly hired Correctional Officer has been given a date to report to work, the investigation is completed after the employee has begun work. It may take several months to over a year to complete an investigation.

Although applicants are hired before their background investigations are conducted, if a discrepancy is found between an applicant's responses during the pre-employment interview and what was discovered during the background investigation, the individual will be asked to explain the discrepancy in writing and may be terminated if found to have been dishonest.

Until 2006, prison staff checked applicants' references with prior employers, extending back 5 years, to verify the employment information and work history applicants provided during their pre-employment interviews. The BOP discontinued the practice in February 2006 because OPM verifies employment information during its background investigation process.

---

[47] The BOP used limited background investigations for Correctional Officers during the time period we reviewed, but has since switched to full background investigations. Limited background investigations include written inquiries covering the most recent 3 years, record searches covering 5 years, and a credit search covering 7 years. Results of the credit search are provided to the requesting agency only if OPM identifies a potential credit problem. Full background investigations extend the written inquiries to cover 5 years. Additionally, OPM provides the requesting agency with the results of the credit search whether there is a potential credit problem or not.

Staff Training Academy

Once hired, Correctional Officers complete a 2-week orientation at the prison where they have been assigned. They then must attend and graduate from the BOP's 3-week Staff Training Academy at the Federal Law Enforcement Training Center in Glynco, Georgia. Continued employment at the BOP is conditional on graduating from the Staff Training Academy. New hires remain on a probationary status for a period of 1 year after their entry-on-duty date.

Background Investigation Adjudication

When OPM completes the background investigation, the BOP's Security and Background Investigation Section adjudicates any discrepancies that have arisen in the individual's background information. Although OPM raises any derogatory issues it has discovered when performing an investigation, SBIS conducts its own evaluation of the investigation's results and may or may not conclude that an issue raised by OPM is of concern. Similarly, SBIS may deem an issue not raised by OPM as a negative factor.

If SBIS finds a discrepancy between information found in the background investigation and what the applicant told the BOP interviewer during the pre-employment interview, and such information would have barred the person from being hired under the Guidelines of Acceptability, it will, in writing, formally ask the individual questions relating to the topic. These questions are known as interrogatories. Answers to these questions determine whether a Correctional Officer will be retained or terminated. In rare cases, the Correctional Officer's Warden may request a waiver of the Guidelines of Acceptability. Such a waiver must be supported by the BOP Regional Director.

Not all background investigations are adjudicated before Correctional Officers reach the end of their 12-month probationary period and become tenured. Terminating a Correctional Officer based upon derogatory information uncovered during a background investigation is a more difficult and lengthier process after the probationary period ends because tenured employees have full collective bargaining unit appeal rights. Although BOP staff have unofficial goals for completing background investigations in less than a year, no official policy states that this must be done.

The OIG sent questionnaires to 18 state departments of corrections (DOC) to collect information about the types of hiring and screening practices they used. Below are selected results of our survey.

Table 8: Type of Employment Screening Performed by the BOP and 18 State Departments of Corrections Surveyed

Type of employment screening	BOP/ state DOCs	Performed?	During pre-employment screening?	During background investigation?
Drug/urinalysis testing	BOP	Yes	Yes	
	State DOCs	18 of 18	Yes	
Psychological evaluation/testing	BOP	No		
	State DOCs	7 of 18	7 of 7	1 of 7*
Polygraph testing	BOP	No		
	State DOCs	No		
NCIC check (criminal history)	BOP	Yes	Yes	
	State DOCs	18 of 18		
Fingerprint check	BOP	Yes	Yes	
	State DOCs	18 of 18		
Financial check	BOP	Yes	Yes	Yes
	State DOCs	3 of 18		3 of 3
Military Service	BOP	Yes	Yes	Ycs
	State DOCs	16 of 18	5 of 18	13 of 16*
Employment history a. Employment verification	BOP	Yes		Yes
	State DOCs	16 of 18	5 of 16	11 of 16
b. Past supervisory or co-worker interviews	BOP	Yes		Yes
	State DOCs	13 of 18	5 of 13	9 of 13*
c. Past job performance evaluations	BOP	No		
	State DOCs	10 of 18	6 of 10	8 of 10*
Driving history	BOP	Yes	Yes	Yes
	State DOCs	18 of 18	8 of 18	13 of 18*

Residential history	BOP	Yes		Yes
	State DOCs	10 of 18	2 of 10	9 of 10*
Substance use history	BOP	Yes	Yes	Yes
	State DOCs	9 of 18	4 of 9	6 of 9*
Personal reference checks	BOP	Yes		Yes
	State DOCs	14 of 18	4 of 14	11 of 14*

* On the survey form, some states checked yes for both pre-employment and background investigation in reporting when they performed this function, therefore there is overlap in the totals. For these states, their background investigation is conducted as part of the pre-employment process, whereas the BOP's pre-employment screening and background investigations are done separately. The BOP's background investigation is initiated after the employee is hired (post employment).

In addition to the categories listed in Table 8 above, the state departments of corrections surveyed listed other methods they use when screening Correctional Officer applicants:

- contacting neighbors,

- domestic violence checks,

- education verification,

- social network checks (for example, Facebook),

- check of contact with current or former inmates through review of visitor databases or the Division of Parole, and

- panel interviews consisting of correctional situational questions.

Many agencies, including the BOP, have thresholds established against which they measure an applicant's suitability for employment. For example, agencies may have written guidelines or policy stating applicants should be eliminated if they have been disciplined or fired from previous employment within a specific timeframe, if they have felony offenses, or if they have used certain illegal substances during a specific timeframe. Table 9 shows the number of states in our survey using the categories of thresholds the BOP uses.

Table 9: Categories of Thresholds Used by the BOP and the State Departments of Corrections to Screen Applicants

Type of screening	Does BOP use specific thresholds?	States that use specific thresholds	States with no thresholds that screen in this category on case-by-case basis	States that do not screen for this category
Criminal history	Yes	18 of 18	0 of 18	0
Employment history	Yes	4 of 18	9 of 18	5
Military history	Yes	6 of 18	5 of 18	7
Driving history	Yes	6 of 18	7 of 18	5
Financial history	Yes	2 of 18	1 of 18	15
Integrity/use of force history	Yes	6 of 18	8 of 18	4
Drug usage history	Yes	8 of 18	5 of 18	5

U.S. Department of Justice

Federal Bureau of Prisons

Office of the Director   Washington, DC 20534

September 21, 2011

MEMORANDUM FOR MICHAEL D. GULLEDGE
                       ASSISTANT INSPECTOR GENERAL FOR
                       EVALUATION AND INSPECTIONS

Thomas R. Kane

FROM: Thomas R. Kane, Acting Director

SUBJECT: Response to the Office of Inspector General's (OIG)
                 Draft Report: <u>Enhanced Screening of BOP
                 Correctional Officer Candidates Could Reduce
                 Likelihood of Misconduct</u>

The Bureau of Prisons (BOP) appreciates the opportunity to respond
to the open recommendation from the draft report entitled <u>Enhanced
Screening of BOP Correctional Officer Candidates Could Reduce
Likelihood of Misconduct</u>.

Please find the Bureau's response to the recommendation below:

Recommendation #1: To reduce the potential for hiring unsuitable
Correctional Officers and thereby to reduce misconduct among
Correctional Officers, OIG recommend that the BOP: Consider
developing a composite scoring mechanism for assessing the
suitability of Correctional Officer applicants.

Response: The BOP concurs with the recommendation to consider a
composite scoring template for applicants. The BOP, working with
the Office of Personnel Management during the past year, is in the
process of piloting a "Core Value Assessment Exam" on applicants at
three BOP institutions. The pilot involves carefully administering
the exam to applicants at federal institutions in Pollock, LA,

U.S. Department of Justice   68
Office of the Inspector General
Evaluation and Inspections Division

Florence, CO, and Victorville, CA, during the pre-employment screening process. By piloting the exam, the BOP and OPM are able to test and then modify the exam to ensure validity before full implementation. The pilot began the week of September 12, 2011, in Pollock and will end in Victorville and Florence the week of September 26, 2011. This exam, once validated and completed in final form, will be given to all applicants and used to screen out applicants who do not adhere to the value system adopted by the BOP. The exam will measure qualities such as integrity, respect, and correctional excellence. We believe it is financially prudent to continue to pursue this effort and measure the outcomes before extending further limited resources to develop another composite scoring mechanism. We anticipate the current pilot of the exam to be completed by September 30, 2011, in order to effectuate any final modifications to the exam before fully utilizing it at all institutions for pre-employment screening in 2012. We request this recommendation be closed.

If you have any questions regarding this response, please contact H. J. Marberry, Assistant Director, Program Review Division, at (202) 353-2302.

APPENDIX VII: OIG ANALYSIS OF THE BOP'S RESPONSE

The Office of the Inspector General provided a draft of this report to the BOP for its comment. The BOP's response is included in Appendix VI to this report. The OIG's analysis of the BOP's response and the actions necessary to close the recommendation are discussed below.

Recommendation. Consider developing a composite scoring mechanism for assessing the suitability of Correctional Officer applicants.

Status. Resolved – open.

Summary of the BOP Response. The BOP concurred with the OIG's recommendation. The BOP stated it is currently piloting a "Core Value Assessment Exam" on applicants at three BOP prisons with the assistance of OPM. The BOP believes it is financially prudent to measure the outcome of this pilot program before embarking on development of additional pre-employment hiring programs. The BOP anticipates completion of the pilot program by September 30, 2011, and utilization of the exam at all BOP prisons by 2012.

OIG Analysis. The actions planned by the BOP are responsive to the OIG's recommendation. By November 30, 2011, please provide a detailed description of the pilot program, elements of the exam relating to composite scoring, results of the pilot program, and plans for implementation of the exam across the BOP in 2012.